William. [from old catalog] Fewsmith, Edgar A. (Edgar Arthur) Singer

An Elementary Grammar Of The English Language

William. [from old catalog] Fewsmith, Edgar A. (Edgar Arthur) Singer

An Elementary Grammar Of The English Language

ISBN/EAN: 9783741134494

Manufactured in Europe, USA, Canada, Australia, Japa

Cover: Foto ©Andreas Hilbeck / pixelio.de

Manufactured and distributed by brebook publishing software (www.brebook.com)

William. [from old catalog] Fewsmith, Edgar A. (Edgar Arthur)
Singer

An Elementary Grammar Of The English Language

AN

ELEMENTARY GRAMMAR

OF THE

ENGLISH LANGUAGE.

BY ... SMITH, A.M.,

... CLASSICAL SCHOOL

... GER,

... GRAMMAR SCHOOL,

AUTHOR OF ... "ENGLISH LANGUAGE."

PHILADELPHIA:
SOWER, BARNES & POTTS,
530 MARKET ST.

Entered according to Act of Congress, in the year 1867, by
SOWER, BARNES & POTTS,
in the Clerk's Office of the District Court of the United States for the
Eastern District of Pennsylvania.

STEREOTYPED BY L. JOHNSON & CO.
PHILADELPHIA.
PRINTED BY SHERMAN & CO.

PREFACE.

This book is, as its name designates, elementary in design and execution. It has been prepared with special reference to the abilities and the wants of those commencing the study of Grammar. Therefore only definitions and principles of primary importance are given, while the illustrations, and the exercises for explaining and inculcating them, are of a simple and familiar character.

The definitions are expressed in the same language as that used in the larger work to which this is intended to be preliminary. By this means, a progressive and consistent series is established, and, in passing from the lower and simpler to the higher and fuller, the learner's first effort of memorizing will also be the last, as it will not be necessary to unlearn in one that which will have been learned in the other: thus the teacher's labor in explaining the more extended application of the principles in the advanced work, will be materially lightened.

The "Introduction" is intended mainly for oral instruction, being designed for such pupils as are not fully prepared to enter into the details of the science. In this part, therefore, all technicalities are avoided, the object being to show the distinctions in the meaning and the use of words, and to derive therefrom appropriate names and a proper classification.

It is desirable, and it is earnestly recommended, that the attention of those commencing the study of Grammar should be directed to material objects, their names, their qualities, their actions, their relations, etc.; pupils will then be prepared to deduce from what will have been thus learned through the senses, those principles which apply to what is abstract.

The treatment of the Sentence in the Introduction will, it is hoped, be found adapted to the understanding of the beginner.

In the main body of the work the division of Grammar into four parts is maintained, but Punctuation and Figures are omitted in Syntax, and all of Prosody is excluded, as not necessary to the scope and the design of this book.

PHILADELPHIA, January 2, 1867.

CONTENTS.

	PAGE
INTRODUCTION	9
GRAMMAR, Definition and Division of	34

PART I.—ORTHOGRAPHY.

LETTERS, Classes of	35
Words	38
Spelling	38
Rules of	39

PART II.—ETYMOLOGY.

CLASSES OF WORDS	41
Parts of Speech, Definitions of	41
NOUNS, Classes of	44
Properties of	45
Number	45
Formation of the Plural	45
Person	48
Gender	49
Case	50
Declension of	51
Parsing, Exercise in	53
PRONOUNS	54
Classes of	55
Personal	55
Compound Personal	56
Relative	58
Compound Relative	59
Interrogative	60
ARTICLES	61
ADJECTIVES	62
Classes of	62
Pronominal	64
Comparison of	65

CONTENTS.

	PAGE
VERBS	68
Classes of, according to Meaning	69
Properties of	70
Voice	70
Mode	72
Tense	73
Number and Person	76
Participles	76
Classes of, according to Formation	78
List of Irregular Verbs	79
Auxiliary, Uses of	83
Conjugation of	84
To Be	84
To Love, Active Voice	87
To Love, Passive Voice	90
ADVERBS	94
Classes of	94
Comparison of	95
PREPOSITIONS	97
Classes of	97
CONJUNCTIONS	99
Classes of	99
INTERJECTIONS	100

PART III.—SYNTAX.

	PAGE
SENTENCES, Definition of	101
Classes of, according to Use	101
Classes of, according to Form	102
DIVISIONS OF SYNTAX	104
Analysis	105
Distinctions of Subject and Predicate	106
Simple Subject and Simple Predicate	106
Complex Subject and Complex Predicate	107
Compound Subject and Compound Predicate	107
Secondary Parts	108
Connecting Parts	108
Independent Parts	108
Qualifications of Simple Subject	110
Qualifications of Simple Predicate	110, 111
Phrases and Clauses	112

CONTENTS.

	PAGE
Synthesis	114
Rule I.—The Subject of a Finite Verb	114
Rule II.—The Nominative Case Independent	115
Rule III.—The Possessive Case	117
Rule IV.—The Objective Case	119
Rule V.—Apposition	120
Rule VI.—Same Case after Verbs	122
Rule VII.—Personal Pronouns	123
Rule VIII.—Relative Pronouns	125
Rule IX.—Articles	127
Rule X.—Adjectives	129
Rule XI.—Pronominal Adjectives	130
Rule XII.—Agreement of Finite Verbs	132
Rule XIII.—Infinitives	135
Rule XIV.—Participles	137
Rule XV.—Adverbs	139
Rule XVI.—Prepositions	141
Rule XVII.—Conjunctions	142
Rule XVIII.—Interjections	144
General Rule	144
General Exercise	145

AN ELEMENTARY ENGLISH GRAMMAR.

INTRODUCTION.

GRAMMAR is the science which treats of the correct use of language.

Science means the principles of any branch of knowledge arranged according to a system, or in regular order.

Principles are *first things*, and are therefore the *most important things*.

All branches of knowledge are built up from first things or principles, just as a house is built up from its foundation.

It is necessary to know these first things, in order to understand exactly very many other things or facts which proceed from them.

When these most important facts, and those which proceed from them, are taken together and arranged properly, they form what is called a *science*.

Thus, *Arithmetic* is the *science of numbers;* *Grammar* is the *science of language*.

LANGUAGE is the means by which human beings express or tell their thoughts to each other.

God gave man not only a mind with which to think, but he gave him also the power of *speech;* that is, the power to express his thoughts by means of *words*.

Words used by man to express thought, form language.

At first all men used or spoke the same language; afterwards, when there came to be various nations or tribes, each nation had words peculiar to itself.

Each of these different sets of words formed a new language; and, as there are a great many different nations, so there are many different languages.

Some nations are rude and barbarous; others have become civilized and enlightened.

Barbarous nations have only a *spoken* language; while enlightened nations have both a *spoken* and a *written* language.

The inhabitants of enlightened nations are therefore able to express their thoughts to each other by means of written or printed, as well as by spoken words.

The people of the United States, the English, the Germans, the French, and some others, are enlightened nations.

The Germans use the German language both in speaking and in writing; the French use the French language; the English, and the most of the inhabitants of the United States, use the English language.

The principles of the different written languages are explained by different grammars, such as German Grammar, French Grammar, English Grammar, etc.

ENGLISH GRAMMAR is the science which treats of the correct use of the English language, both in speaking and in writing.

When we speak, or use spoken language, we utter *sounds*.

In *spoken language*, the simplest sound which can be made or uttered, is called an *elementary* sound.

In *written language*, these sounds themselves can not be written or printed, but certain marks can be made which *represent* them, or which *serve as signs* of them.

The marks or signs used to represent certain sounds of the human voice are called *Letters*.

Different written languages have different letters. All the letters of any language form the *alphabet* of that language.

INTRODUCTION. 11

In the English alphabet, the letters *a, e, i, o,* and *u,* and sometimes *w* and *y,* are called *Vowels.*

All the other letters are called *Consonants.*

Two or more letters may be so combined as to form, when uttered, but one sound; as, *up, up-on.*

This combination of letters is called a *Syllable.*

A single letter may sometimes form a syllable; as, *a* in the word *a-ble.*

Two or more syllables properly combined form what is called a *Word.* One syllable may be a word; as, *man.*

WORDS.

A *Word* is a letter, or a number of letters, used to express some idea.

A *Spoken Word* is a sound, or a number of sounds combined, used to express some idea.

A *Written Word* is a letter, or a number of letters combined, used as the *sign* of an idea; as, *a, tree, summer, commander.*

As words are used to express ideas or thoughts, a great many words are required to express all the thoughts that may arise in the mind.

In the English language, there are many thousand words.

Although there are so many words in our language, they may be arranged in *nine classes* or *kinds,* according to the use or the meaning of each word.

THE CLASSES OF WORDS.

The names of the *Nine Classes of Words* are, NOUN, PRONOUN, ARTICLE, ADJECTIVE, VERB, ADVERB, PREPOSITION, CONJUNCTION, and INTERJECTION.

In order to know to which class any word belongs, it is necessary to know its meaning, and to know how it is used.

NOUNS.

All things that we can see, feel, hear, taste, smell, or think of, have names. Such things may be called *objects*.

The words which are used as the names of objects are called *Nouns*.

A NOUN is a word used as the name of any thing; as, *log, dress, goodness, heat.*

EXERCISE I.—Notice ten objects which you can now see.
Mention the names of those objects.
What are the words used as the names of those objects called? Why?
Mention the names of ten objects which you can taste or smell.
What are the words used as the names of those objects called? Why?
Mention the names of ten objects which you can not see, hear, feel, taste, or smell, but of which you can think.
What are the words used as the names of those objects called? Why?

EXERCISE II.—[*Objects* themselves can not be written, but their *names* can be written. The names of boys and girls, and of cities, towns, rivers, etc., should each be commenced with a capital letter.]

Write ten names of boys;—of girls;—of great or good men;—of places;—of good habits;—of bad habits;—of flowers;—of metals;—of cities or towns;—of animals;—of trees;—of rivers.

To what class of words do those which you have written belong? Why? Can we *write objects?* Can we *write* the *names* of objects? What names must each be commenced with a capital letter?

EXERCISE III.—Mention the *nouns* in the following sentences, and tell why each is a noun:—

MODEL.—"God creates."

God.—"God" is a noun; it is a noun because it is a word used as a name.

1. The scholars learn. 2. The ship sinks. 3. George reads. 4. The grass grows. 5. Idleness displeases. 6. Hear the noise. 7. The day is bright. 8. Wisdom is precious. 9. Acquire good habits. 10. The boy's hat was lost. 11. America was discovered by Columbus. 12. Children, obey your parents. 13. The wolf and the sheep drank from the same stream. 14. The heat of the sun melts the ice and the snow. 15. Drunkenness is a vice which all should despise. 16. The winds blew,

and the rains fell, and beat upon that house. 17. The tiger is a strong animal; but it is not equal to the lion in strength. 18. The stars twinkle in the sky. 19. Oranges, lemons, and pine-apples grow in hot countries. 20. Apples, pears, and peaches are produced in temperate climates. 21. Early one summer morning, before the family were stirring, an old clock, that, without giving its owner any cause of complaint, had stood for fifty years in a farmer's kitchen, suddenly stopped.

PRONOUNS.

It would seem awkward, and it would be very tiresome, to mention the name of an object about which we speak very often, every time we refer to that object.

Thus, the expression, "John said that John loved John's parents," is a very clumsy one, because John's name is repeated so often.

The sentence would be much better thus:—"John said that *he* loved *his* parents." Here, for the noun *John*, the word *he* is used; and for the noun *John's*, *his* is used.

So, also, instead of saying, "Mary lost Mary's books and could not find the books," it would be better to say, "Mary lost *her* books and could not find *them*."

In the two improved sentences, *he, his, her,* and *them*, are used *for nouns* or *in place of nouns.*

All words that are used in place of nouns are called *Pronouns,* a word which means *for nouns.*

A PRONOUN is a word used in place of a noun; as, "The *snow* melts as *it* falls into the stream."

If John were speaking and wished to say that he himself had been reading, he would not say, "*John* has been reading;" he would say, "*I* have been reading."

What word is here used in place of the name of the person speaking? To what class of words does it belong? Why?

In place of the name of one person speaking, we use the pronoun *I, my, mine,* or *me.*

If more than one are speaking, *we, our, ours,* or *us,* is used.

If John were speaking to James and wished to say that James had been playing, he would not say, "James has been playing;" he would say, "*You* have been playing."

What word is here used in place of the name of the person spoken to? To what class of words does it belong? Why?

In place of the name of one person spoken to, we use the pronoun *thou, thy, thine, thee, you, your*, or *yours*. If more than one are spoken to, *you, your*, or *yours*, is used.

If John were speaking to James about Henry, he would not say, "Henry was playing, but Henry stopped;" he would say, "Henry was playing, but *he* stopped."

What word is here used in place of the name of the person spoken of? To what class of words does it belong? Why?

In place of the name of one man, one boy, etc., spoken of, we use the pronoun *he, his*, or *him*. If more than one are spoken of, *they, their, theirs*, or *them*, is used.

In place of the name of one woman, one girl, etc., spoken of, we use the pronoun *she, her*, or *hers*. If more than one are spoken of, *they, their, theirs*, or *them*, is used.

In place of the name of one thing without life spoken of, we use *it*, or *its*. If more than one are spoken of, *they, their, theirs*, or *them*, is used.

In the list of pronouns, it will be noticed, different pronouns are used for the name of the person speaking, the person spoken to, and the person spoken of.

EXERCISE I.—What pronouns may be used for the name of one person speaking? What pronouns may be used if more than one are speaking?

What pronouns may be used for the name of one person spoken to? What pronouns may be used if more than one are spoken to?

INTRODUCTION. 15

What pronouns may be used for the name of one man, etc., spoken of?—of one woman, etc., spoken of?—of one thing without life spoken of?

What pronouns may be used if more than one man, woman, or thing without life, are spoken of?

EXERCISE II.—Use a proper pronoun instead of repeating a noun in each of the following sentences:—

"Mary lost Mary's cloak."

MODEL.—In place of the noun *Mary's*, the pronoun *her* should be used, and the sentence should be, "Mary lost her cloak."

1. George forgets George's lesson. 2. Charles said that Charles was tired. 3. Edwin has mislaid Edwin's knife. 4. George and William lost George's and William's books. 5. James, will James come here? 6. Mary can do well if Mary will try. 7. The river is narrow, but the river is deep. 8. The vessels fired a salute as the vessels passed the fort. 9. The boy lost the boy's way, and the boy lay in the woods all night. 10. Bees gather bees' honey in the summer, and store honey away for bees' use in the winter. 11. Children should try to please children's parents in all things.

To what class of words does each word used in place of a noun belong?

EXERCISE III.—Use the proper pronoun in each of the following blanks:—

1. The boy struck — sister, and hurt — very much. 2. A cloud passed under the sun and hid —. 3. Some birds build — nests on the ground. 4. Beavers build — houses by the side of some stream. 5. When the travelers had rested, — continued — journey. 6. Boys, do not let — passions control —. 7. Some animals are killed for — fur. 8. The old beggar wanted some food, for — was very hungry. 9. Victoria is loved by — subjects. 10. Every boy can become a good man if — will try. 11. God makes — sun to shine on the just and on the unjust. 12. The tree lay where — fell.

For what noun has the pronoun in each sentence been used? What is a pronoun?

EXERCISE IV.—Mention each *pronoun* in the following sentences, and tell for what noun it is used:—

"The roses have lost their beauty."

MODEL.—*Their*.—"Their" is a pronoun; it is a pronoun because it is a word used in place of the noun *roses*.

1. The bird sings because it is happy. 2. Love a friend and never forsake him. 3. Thomas, I have seen your cousin; he is well. 4. The eagle has his home in the mountain. 5. The cow and her calf were both sold. 6. When spring comes, trees put forth their leaves. 7. Samuel

studies his lesson at home. 8. Speak the truth and you will be respected. 9. The basket had four eggs in it. 10. The stag will not stand still when he sees a man or a dog. 11. Bees live in a hive; they work hard. 12. Ann, will you let us play with your toys?

EXERCISE V.—Write in one column the nouns in the last exercise, and in another column the pronouns which stand for them.

Write in a third column the nouns which have no pronouns standing for them.

ARTICLES.

If we speak of an object by merely mentioning its name, as, *tree, apple, horse*, it is not always known whether any *particular* tree, apple, or horse is meant, or not.

For the purpose of showing whether or not any particular object or objects are meant, the words *a*, *an*, and *the* may be used.

Thus, in the expression, *a tree*, *a* is used to denote *one* tree of a number of trees, but it does not denote any particular tree; it does not limit the meaning of the word *tree* to any particular object.

Also in the sentence, "Give me an apple," I do not mean to ask for a particular apple; any apple will suit.

But in the sentence, "The horse was stolen," the word *the* shows that a particular horse is meant; it limits the meaning of the word *horse* to some particular object.

The words *a*, *an*, and *the* are called *Articles*.

An ARTICLE is the word *the*, or *a* or *an*, which is used before a noun to limit its meaning; as, *a* horse, *an* ounce, *the* river.

A is used before a word which, when spoken, begins with a consonant sound; as, *a* man, *a* union.

An is used instead of *a*, before a word which, when spoken, begins with a vowel sound; as, *an* east wind; *an* honest man.

The may be used before a spoken word beginning with either a vowel or a consonant sound; as, *the* east, *the* north.

EXERCISE I.—Use *the* before each of the following nouns:—
Edge, curls, bush, sparrows, father, pleasures, unit, odors.

Use properly *a* or *an* before each of the following nouns, and tell why it should be used:—
Ode, song, deed, act, prince, expense, wish, union, claim, egg, stand, evening, arbor, bower.

To what class of words does *a* or *an* belong? Why?—*the?* Why?

EXERCISE II.—Use properly *a* or *an* in the following sentences, and tell why it should be used:—

1. Honeysuckles grew by the door of — humble dwelling. 2. — honest man is God's best work. 3. They rode for — hour and then rested. 4. — unit is the smallest number. 5. — united people can not be conquered. 6. — ant-hill was seen on — hill. 7. — orange was bought for the sick child. 8. — wonderful change took place. 9. The event happened at — evil hour.

What is an article?

EXERCISE III.—Mention each *article* in the following sentences, and tell why it is an article:—

"A knife was lost."

MODEL.—*A.*—"A" is an article; it is an article because it is a word used to limit the meaning of the noun *knife;* it shows that no particular knife is meant.

1. In an hour there are sixty minutes. 2. The beasts and the birds have gone to their shelter. 3. What is the use of an eye, if it is not employed? 4. The squirrel makes a hole in an old tree and lives in it. 5. The world upon which we live is a large ball. 6. The eyes of an eagle can gaze at the bright sun. 7. The sword-fish is a curious creature.

EXERCISE IV.—Write in separate columns the nouns, the pronouns, and the articles, in the preceding sentences.

ADJECTIVES.

Certain words are used to denote the shape, the color, the number, the size, etc. of objects: thus, a *round* ball; a *green* leaf; *fifty* miles; the *largest* apple.

If we say, "A *sweet* apple," we mean that the apple has or possesses the *quality of sweetness.*

INTRODUCTION.

We can not speak or write the *quality* of any thing; that is in the thing itself; but a word can be used which will *denote* that quality: thus, the word *good* denotes the quality *goodness;* the word *hot* denotes the quality *heat.*

A word that *denotes some quality* of an object is said to *describe* that object.

We can not speak or write *number,* but words can be used which will *denote* the number of any object or objects: thus, *five* denotes number.

A word that *denotes some number* of any object or objects is said to *limit* that object or those objects.

A word used with the name of an object to denote some quality or number respecting that object, is called an *Adjective.*

An ADJECTIVE is a word used to describe or to limit a noun or a pronoun; as, the *rich* man; *ten* dollars; he is *good.*

Such words as *good, bad, obedient, sweet, sour, happy, bright, virtuous, red, green,* and a great many others, are adjectives which *describe.*

Such words as *one, two, first, second, single, double, twofold, each, any, all, many, other,* etc., are adjectives which *limit.*

EXERCISE I.—Use with each of the following nouns and pronouns a word which will describe or limit it:—

Trees, flowers, buds, horse, cow, book, slate, pencil, city, lamp, river, day, night, cloud, beauty, George, queen, Jane, sky, he, she, president, iron, they.

What is a word which describes or limits a noun or a pronoun called?

EXERCISE II.—Use each of the following words to describe or limit a noun or a pronoun:—

Happy, obedient, double, truthful, straight, largest, excellent, best, lovely, northern, fewer, black, cleaner, industrious, lazy, lonely, troublesome, twenty, triple, foolish, beloved, unknown, hard-working, fifty-five.

To what class of words does a word which describes or limits a noun or a pronoun belong?

Describe each object which you may see in this room by using an adjective with the name of that object.

EXERCISE III.—Use an *adjective* in place of each blank in the following sentences:—

1. The valley lay between — mountains. 2. A — house stood on the hill-side. 3. I have a very — home. 4. Charles's — temper caused — unhappiness to his parents. 5. You should be —, and —, and — to every body. 6. Her — ringlets, and — cheeks, and — eyes, excited admiration. 7. A righteous man is as — as a lion. 8. — pecks make — bushel. 9. The — child played upon the — beach. 10. — words stir up anger. 11. A walk along the — lane is —, when the —, — day draws to a close. 12. Henry still looked —, though he was much —.

EXERCISE IV.—Mention the *adjectives* in each of the following sentences, and tell why each is an adjective:—

"A soft answer turneth away wrath."

MODEL 1.—*Soft*.—"Soft" is an adjective; it is an adjective because it is a word used to describe the noun *answer*.

"The first snow has fallen."

2.—*First*.—"First" is an adjective; it is an adjective because it is a word used to limit the noun *snow*.

1. Bright eyes sparkle. 2. Sweet sounds soothe the ear. 3. Grievous words stir up anger. 4. The hungry lion roars. 5. Ten cents make one dime. 6. The two men lost their way. 7. The green leaves wither. 8. The Holy Bible teaches heavenly wisdom. 9. He is happy, but I am sad. 10. How bright and beautiful are the flowers on a May morning! 11. On an autumn night a high wind blew, and a heavy rain fell. 12. The coarsest food tastes good to a hungry man. 13. The morning bright, with rosy light, has waked me up from sleep.

EXERCISE V.—Write in one column the adjectives in the preceding sentences, and in another, the nouns and the pronouns which they describe or limit.

Write also in separate columns the other nouns and pronouns, and the articles.

VERBS.

We can not speak of any thing without saying that it *does* something, or that it *acts;* or else that it has *existence* or *being;* or else that it is in some *condition* or *state*.

Thus, in the sentence, "The bird flies," the word *flies* is used to *assert*, or *declare*, or *say* that the bird *does* something, or that it *acts*.

In the sentence, "The boy is here," the word *is* is used to *assert* that the boy has *being* or *existence* here.

In the sentence, "John sleeps," the word *sleeps* is used to *assert* that John is in a certain *state*.

A word which asserts the action, the being, or the state of any thing is called a *Verb*.

A VERB is a word used to assert action, being, or state; as, "The boy *killed* a bird."—"They *have been* away."—"William *lies* on the grass."

Two, three, or even four words, are often taken together as forming one verb.

Thus, in the sentences, "The horse has eaten," "James may have gone," and "He might have been hurt," *has eaten, may have gone,* and *might have been hurt,* are verbs.

Verbs are the most important words in the language, because no sentence can be made to express complete sense without the use of a verb.

EXERCISE I.—Mention twenty words which express action; such as *run, sing,* etc.

Mention five words which express being, or state; as, *is, rests,* etc.

[The action, the being, or the state of any thing can not be written, but words expressing that action, being, or state can be written.]

Write five words used to assert action, concerning *boy:* thus, "The boy *runs,*" etc.

Write five words asserting action, being, or state, of the farmer;—of the merchant;—of the sailor;—of *he ;*—of soldiers;—of animals;—of birds;—of *they ;*—of lessons;—of money;—of wisdom;—of idleness;—of cities;—of ships;—of good men.

To what class of words does each word which expresses action belong?—each word which expresses being or state?

EXERCISE II.—Use a suitable verb to complete each of the following sentences:—

1. The sun —. 2. The snow — on the mountain. 3. I — my book. 4. The oak — a noble tree. 5. Houses — of brick or stone. 6. He — to the ground and — himself. 7. The ship — across the ocean. 8. The light — through glass. 9. Carpenters — houses. 10. He — the ball and — it against the house. 11. Oranges — in warm countries. 12. Coal —

— in the hilly regions of Pennsylvania. 13. Sheep — — for their wool 14. Some books — pretty stories. 15. The boys — to see their cousins who — in the country. 16. Kind words — the heavy heart. 17. Indians only lived in America when it — —. 18. The flowers which — — yesterday — —.

Tell why the words used in the blanks are verbs.

EXERCISE III.—Name each *verb* in the following sentences, and tell why it is a verb:—

"He has finished his work."

MODEL.—*Has finished.*—"Has finished," is a verb; it is a verb because it is a word used to assert action.

1. They were frightened. 2. The soldiers surrounded the house. 3. The farmer sows the seed and reaps the grain. 4. He found the place. 5. The place was found. 6. The soldier lost his life. 7. He might have been loved. 8. The river overflowed its banks. 9. A pretty brook runs through the meadow. 10. Idle boys should learn a lesson from the busy bees. 11. Flora was fond of the lovely flowers. 12. Little drops of water make the mighty ocean. 13. The boy and his sister played together. 14. Flowers soon fade, and wither and die. 15. Children should store their minds with knowledge. 16. Clocks and watches measure time. 17. Twenty-four hours make a day. 18. Blackbirds steal the farmer's corn.

EXERCISE IV.—Write in one column the nouns found in all the sentences in the last Exercise.

In separate columns write all the pronouns and all the adjectives in the last Exercise.

ADVERBS.

In the sentence, "The train moves swiftly," the word *swiftly* is used to show in *what manner* the action expressed by the verb *moves* takes place.

Some words are used to denote the *place* of an action; as, "The ball struck *there.*"

Words are also used to express the *time* of an action; as, 'The train moved *immediately.*"

In the sentences given above, the words *swiftly*, *there*, and *immediately* are adverbs.

The word *adverb* means *to a verb*, and is so called because an adverb is usually *joined to a verb*, or is *used with a verb* to show the *time*, the *place*, or the *manner* of an action.

An adverb may express *how* or in *what degree* the quality denoted by an *adjective* is considered; as, "He is a *very bad* boy."

An adverb may also be used to vary or qualify the meaning of *another adverb;* as, "The bird flew *very swiftly.*"

A word which denotes the time, the place, or the manner of an action expressed by a verb, or which varies or qualifies the meaning of an adjective or of an adverb, is called an *Adverb.*

An ADVERB is a word used to qualify the meaning of a verb, an adjective, or another adverb; as, "The scholar studies *industriously.*"—"James learned a *very* difficult lesson."—"*How eagerly* he hurried *back!*"

Such words as *always, daily, ever, lately, now, never, often, seldom, then, yesterday,* etc., are adverbs of *time.*

Such words as *hence, here, hither, out, there, thither, where, nowhere, somewhere, yonder,* etc., are adverbs of *place.*

Such words as *so, thus, well, badly, easily, somehow, certainly, truly, roughly, smoothly,* etc., are adverbs of *manner.*

Some of the adverbs which qualify adjectives or other adverbs are *almost, altogether, ever, much, more, less, not, so, very.*

EXERCISE I.—With each of the following verbs use five words which will denote the time of the action; as, "James runs *now;*"—five which will denote the place; as, "He works *there;*"—five, which will denote the manner; as, "She sings *sweetly.*"

Run, walk, read, eat, heard, will come, has gone, listened, see, shines, grow, whistle, speak, hide, had written, declare.

With each of the following adjectives use words which will qualify its meaning; as, *truly* noble:—

Good, wise, bad, foolish, industrious, honest, lively, uneven, lazy, clean, ripe, sour, strange, thoughtful, plain.

With each of the following adverbs use other adverbs, which will qualify its meaning:—Quietly, often, wisely, foolishly, fiercely, well.

To what class of words does a word which denotes the time, the place, or the manner of an action, or which qualifies the meaning of an adjective or an adverb, belong?

INTRODUCTION. 23

EXERCISE II.—Use an appropriate adverb in place of each blank in the following sentences:—

1. He has — finished his work. 2. The men work —. 3. The rain falls —. 4. The snow fell — to the ground. 5. He is — a — good scholar. 6. Solomon was a — wise man. 7. Glass is a — brittle metal. 8. I have seen him —. 9. I do not know — the mistake happened. 10. Speak the truth —. 11. How — the birds sing when the sun shines —. 12. The boat sailed — into port. 13. He who rises — loses the best part of the day. 14. He rode — than we. 15. Read — if you would read —.

EXERCISE III.—Name the *adverbs* in the following sentences, and tell why each is an adverb:—

"He soon returned to his home."

MODEL.—*Soon.*—"Soon" is an adverb; it is an adverb because it is a word used to denote the time of the action expressed by the verb *returned.*

1. Commence your labor now, and it will soon be finished. 2. Sparks fly upward. 3. The party returned sooner than we expected. 4. Never do a mean action. 5. Live honestly, and you will not want. 6. The brook danced noisily over the pebbly bottom. 7. He bitterly repented of his bad act. 8. You are certainly foolish if you waste your time. 9. They do not recite very well. 10. They divided the apples equally. 11. A boy can not become suddenly bad. 12. Corn grows rapidly in rich soil. 13. Speak truthfully, and you will always be believed.

EXERCISE IV.—Write in separate columns the nouns, the pronouns, the adjectives, and the verbs in Exercise III.

PREPOSITIONS.

Certain words are used to show a connection between two things; and they usually compare the time or the place of one with that of the other.

Thus, in the sentence, "The book on the desk is mine," the word *on* connects the idea denoted by the word *book,* with the idea denoted by the word *desk;* — it suggests the place of the book with regard to the desk; that is, the book is *on* the desk, not *under* it, nor *by* it, nor *in* it.

A word which connects the ideas denoted by two words, and compares them with regard to time or place, is said to *show relation* between them.

Such a word may show the relation between two objects or

their names; between an object and an action expressed by a verb; or between a noun or a pronoun following it and some preceding word.

A word which shows relation between a noun or a pronoun and some preceding word is called a *Preposition*.

A PREPOSITION is a word used before a noun or a pronoun to show its relation to some preceding word; as, "They sat *under* the tree."—"The blame rests *upon* him."

There are about fifty prepositions in the language. Nineteen of them are called *simple* prepositions; they are *at, after, by, down, for, from, in, on, of, over, past, round, since, through, till, to, under, up,* and *with*.

Thirteen commence with the syllable *a;* as, *aboard, above, across, against, along,* etc.

Nine commence with the syllable *be;* as, *before, behind, below, beneath,* etc.

Ten are formed by uniting two prepositions or a preposition and an adverb; as, *into, throughout, upon,* etc.

EXERCISE I.—How many prepositions are there?
How many are simple prepositions? Mention some of them.
Name the three ways of forming those prepositions that are not simple prepositions.
Mention three prepositions formed in the first way;—three formed in the second;—three formed in the third.
Between what does a preposition show relation?

EXERCISE II.—Use an appropriate preposition in each of the following sentences:—

1. Victoria is queen — England. 2. The house was shaken — the wind. 3. It is pleasant to roam — the forests — the warm days — summer. 4. A voyage — the ocean is sometimes dangerous. 5. News can now be sent — the United States — Europe — the telegraph — the ocean. 6. The boy seemed bent — mischief. 7. The thief attempted to rob him — his money. 8. The river abounds — fish. 9. Reflect often — your conduct. 10. Depend — your own exertions and not — th

exertions — others. 11. The robin flew — the tree and hid itself — the branches.

EXERCISE III.—Name each *preposition* in the following sentences, and tell why it is a preposition:—

"The train ran over the boy."

MODEL.—*Over.*—"Over" is a preposition; it is a preposition because it is a word used before the noun *boy* to show its relation to the verb *ran*.

1. Two boys went into the woods one day, and hunted for a bird's nest; they soon found one on a low branch of a tree, with the bird on the nest. 2. One boy crept behind the tree and caught the bird ere it could fly from the nest. The other boy took the nest, which had four blue eggs in it, and then they started for home. 3. While they were going home they began to quarrel about the nest, because each wished it for himself. While they struggled, the bird flew away from them, and they trod upon the eggs in the nest and broke them.

EXERCISE IV.—Write in one column the prepositions in the preceding sentences; in a column on the right hand write the nouns or the pronouns before which the prepositions are placed; on the left, the words to which they show the relation of the nouns or the pronouns.

In separate columns write the nouns, the pronouns, the adjectives, the verbs, and the adverbs, in the last Exercise.

CONJUNCTIONS.

"Apples are ripe and pears are ripe." This sentence is made up of two shorter sentences, of which "Apples are ripe" is one, and "pears are ripe" is the other.

These two sentences are connected or united, or made one, by the use of the word *and*.

These two sentences can be united so as to make a shorter sentence than the one first given: thus, "Apples and pears are ripe."

By omitting the words *are ripe* after the word *apples, and* is made to connect the words *apples* and *pears;* and it also prevents the repetition of parts which are alike in both sentences.

A word which connects sentences, parts of a sentence, or words, is called a *Conjunction*.

A CONJUNCTION is a word used to connect the words, the parts of a sentence, or the sentences, between which it is placed; as, "Let us be kind, *and* just, *and* good."—"Do not annoy *or* vex your friends,"

The following are some of the principal conjunctions:— *And, as, also, although, because, both, but, either, for, if, neither, nor, or, since, so, than, that, then,* and *yet.*

A conjunction connects two or more words which belong to the same class of words; that is, it connects two or more nouns, two or more pronouns, two or more adjectives, etc.

EXERCISE I.—Name the principal conjunctions. What is a conjunction?
What kinds of words only can conjunctions connect?

EXERCISE II.—Use an appropriate conjunction in each of the following sentences:—
1. Winter soon passes, — spring returns. 2. His brother came, — he did not remain. 3. The scholar was late, — he had played on his way. 4. His little brother — sister were not able — to read — to write. 5. The lame boy can not run — play as you — I can. 6. James was a good boy, — he could not learn his lessons as well — his classmates. 7. Boys bait their hooks with flies — worms. 8. Study now, — you will not always have a chance to do so. 9. Our words — our deeds should always agree. 10. Let your words be few — to the point.
What are the words used to connect words, parts of a sentence, or sentences, called?

EXERCISE III.—Name each *conjunction* in the following sentences, and tell why it is a conjunction:—
"We might all learn if we would study."
MODEL.—*If.*—"If" is a conjunction; it is a conjunction because it is a word used to connect the two sentences, *We might learn* and *we would study.*
1. Labor and rest are as day and night are. 2. I will get the book if you wish it. 3. The little fellow suffered, although he did not complain. 4. The horse was frightened because he heard the noise of the cannon. 5. Neither wisdom nor fame can be gained without labor. 6. The stars are very far off, but their distances can be measured. 7. The poor boy can not run, nor play, nor jump as he once could.
8. In the daytime, the rabbit lies in its burrow, but in the night it

INTRODUCTION. 27

comes and hops around for food; it feeds on herbs and plants in the summer, but in the winter, when there are no green herbs, it feeds on buds, twigs, or on the bark of young trees.

EXERCISE IV.—Write the conjunctions in the last Exercise, and the words which they connect.

Write also in separate columns all the nouns, the pronouns, the adjectives, the verbs, the adverbs, and the prepositions, in the preceding sentences.

INTERJECTIONS.

There are a few words which express joy; such as, *Aha! hurrah!* etc.

Some express sorrow; as, *Oh! alas!* etc.

Some express a desire for silence; as, *Hush! hist! whist!* etc.

A word used in sudden calling out, or to express joy, or sorrow, or disgust, or laughter, etc., is called an *Interjection*.

An INTERJECTION is a word used in exclamation to express some emotion of the mind; as, *Oh. alas! hush! ha!*

EXERCISE I.—Name the *interjections* in the following sentences, and tell why each is an interjection:—

"Alas! how hard is my fate!"

MODEL—*Alas!*—"Alas" is an interjection; it is an interjection because it is a word used in exclamation to express sorrow.

1. Hush! I hear a noise. 2. Ah! my poor dog is dead. 3. Fie! you should be ashamed of such conduct. 4. Hurrah! we have a holiday. 5. Oh! how sad a story!

EXERCISE II.—Write in separate columns the nouns, the pronouns, the articles, the adjectives, the verbs, the adverbs, the prepositions, and the conjunctions in the last Exercise.

GENERAL EXERCISES.

I.—Write in columns the words belonging to each class of words in the following sentences:—

[Or, if the teacher prefer, simply name the class of words to which each word in the following sentences belongs, and give the reasons, according to the previous models.]

1. A kind word can never die. 2. The pony is in the field, but we can catch him. 3. The cat jumped upon the chair. 4. The hut was built of logs. 5. Bees often make their home in the tops of hollow trees. 6. A big dog ran after Charles, and, alas! bit him severely. 7. Ten dimes make one dollar. 8. The sun's rays dazzled her eyes. 9. Death is ever busy: oh! how insecure is life! 10. We hold a pen between the thumb and the fingers.

11. The Bible is of more value than all the other books in the world: we should therefore study it more than any other book. 12. The cruel man beat his horse with a heavy club. 13. The lady wore an elegant veil. 14. Ellen reads distinctly. 15. A horse is easily guided by a rein. 16. My father and I visited the museum, and we saw many curious sights. 17. A good boy will not be rude in his conduct. 18. Thirty-two quarts are contained in one bushel. 19. Our puss has very sharp claws. 20. A sad accident happened on the railroad; some lives were lost, and many persons were injured.

21. When the ground is covered with snow, the crows come very near to the house. 22. He was quite calm, though he was in great danger. 23. Was he obedient, or disobedient? 24. Hark! how fiercely the wind howls! 25. We will notice the different kinds of trees, and will learn to tell their names, as we walk along the lane. 26. "Here is a visitor for you," said Mary's uncle as he entered the room with a little white mouse in a cage. 27. The letters in books are made by means of types; ink is put upon the types, and then the types are pressed upon the paper. 28. The travelers knew that they would find water there, because the grass looked fresh and green.

II.—[The first word of every sentence should be commenced with a capital A period (.) must be placed at the end of every sentence.]

Compose and write ten sentences, each containing a noun and a verb; —ten, each containing a noun, a pronoun, and a verb.

Compose and write ten sentences, each containing an adjective, a noun, a pronoun, and a verb;—ten, each containing an adjective, a noun, a pronoun, a verb, and an adverb.

Compose and write ten sentences, each containing an adjective, a noun, a pronoun, a verb, an adverb, and a preposition followed by a noun or a pronoun.

Compose and write ten sentences, each containing a conjunction connecting words, parts of a sentence, or sentences;—ten, containing interjections.

SENTENCES.

In the preceding lessons we have considered words separately: we will now consider words as they are arranged to express thoughts.

Two or more words arranged properly and making full sense form what is called a *Sentence.*

A SENTENCE is two or more words so combined as to make complete sense.

Although each of the words *the, rises,* and *sun* has some meaning, yet these words do not fully express a thought unless arranged in a certain order: thus, "The sun rises."

At least two words are needed to form a sentence; one of them must be a name, or a word used for a name, and the other must be a verb.

No sentence can be formed without a verb.

Thus, *Sugar sweet,* or *sweet sugar,* is not full sense: a verb is needed to say or assert something of *sugar:* thus, "Sugar *is* sweet," or "Sugar *tastes* sweet."

No sentence can be formed without something of which the verb asserts action, being, or state.

Thus, *writes* expresses *action;* but to form a sentence, or to make full sense, something is needed about which to *assert* that *action:* thus, "*John* writes."

Also, *sleeps* expresses a *state;* but to form a sentence something is needed about which to *assert* that *state:* thus, "*Mary* or *she* sleeps."

THE PARTS OF SENTENCES.

Every sentence, however short or however long, can be divided into two parts.

One of these parts is called the *Subject;* the other is called the *Predicate.*

No sentence can be formed without these two parts.

THE SUBJECT.

The SUBJECT of a sentence is that of which something is said or asserted.

Thus, in the sentence, "Water flows," *water* is that of which *flows* is asserted. *Water*, then, is the *subject*.

The word *subject* means the *thing of which something is said*.

In the sentence, "The deep water flows," *the deep water* is that of which *flows* is asserted. *The deep water*, then, is the subject of the sentence.

The subject is a noun or a pronoun taken alone, or a noun or a pronoun taken with other words.

In either case this noun or pronoun is called the *subject-nominative*.

Thus, in the sentence, "Water flows," *water* is both the subject and the subject-nominative.

In the sentence, "The deep water flows," *the deep water* is the subject, and the noun *water* taken alone is the subject-nominative.

THE PREDICATE.

The PREDICATE of a sentence is that which is said or asserted of the subject, or about it.

Thus, in the sentence, "Water flows," it is *flows* that is asserted of the subject *water*. *Flows*, then, is the *predicate*.

The word *predicate* means *something said or asserted of*.

Again, in the sentence, "The deep water flows without noise," it is *flows without noise* that is asserted of the subject, *the deep water*. Therefore *flows without noise* is the predicate of the sentence.

The verb in the predicate is called the *predicate-verb*.

In the sentence, "Water flows," *flows* is both the predicate and the predicate-verb.

In the sentence, "The deep water flows without noise," *flows without noise* is the predicate, and *flows* taken alone is the predicate-verb.

EXERCISE.--Mention the *subject* and the *predicate*, also the *subject*.

INTRODUCTION. 31

nominative and the *predicate-verb*, in each of the following sentences, and give the reasons:—

MODEL 1.—" Dogs growl."
In this sentence, *dogs* is the subject, because it is that of which *growl* is said or asserted; and *growl* is the predicate, because it is that which is asserted of the subject *dogs*.

Dogs is the subject-noun or subject-nominative, and *growl* is the predicate-verb.

2.—"The fresh air feels very pleasant."
In this sentence, *the fresh air* is the subject, because it is that of which *feels very pleasant* is asserted; and *feels very pleasant* is the predicate, because it is that which is asserted of the subject, *the fresh air*.

Air is the subject-nominative, and *feels* is the predicate-verb.

1. God is. 2. God is good. 3. He made all things. 4. Willie loves the country. 5. Foxes prowl. 6. Crickets chirp. 7. The ball rolls down the hill. 8. The bright sun warms the earth. 9. Jane has plucked the rose. 10. The red rose is a beautiful flower. 11. The shower of rain has revived the flowers. 12. The tired beggar sits by the wayside. 13. The luscious melons are now ripe. 14. The cunning mice ran into their holes. 15. Good lessons have been recited. 16. A high mountain is before us. 17. We will climb the high mountain. 18. My knife is lost. 19. I have lost my knife. 20. Shame will bring a blush to the cheek. 21. Pleasing manners win attention. 22. A regiment of soldiers contains ten companies. 23. The busy bees improve the sunny hours. 24. How sweetly the birds sing! 25. Very sad consequences sometimes result from a single mistake. 26. Can you guess the riddle? 27. The field of grass has been mowed. 28. The timid deer was startled by his own shadow in the water. 29. The great and good God gives us all our blessings.

The subject sometimes contains two or more subject-nominatives connected by one conjunction or more than one.

Thus, "*You* and *he* may come."—"*Wheat, corn, rye,* and *oats* are raised by the farmers."

The predicate sometimes contains two or more predicate-verbs connected by one conjunction or more than one.

Thus, "You and he *may come* and *may stay* awhile."— "Charles *hops, skips,* and *jumps.*"

EXERCISE.—Mention the *subjects* and the *predicates*, also the *subject-nominatives* and the *predicate-verbs*, in the following sentences:—
1. Day and night succeed each other. 2. Violets and daisies grow along the bank. 3. I love and obey my teacher. 4. The swift hounds caught and killed the cunning fox at last. 5. Silks and calicoes are sold here. 6. Boots and shoes are worn by men and boys. 7. The farmer ploughs and sows his fields. 8. Blackboards, maps, slates, pencils, and inkstands are necessary in a school-room. 9. Theodore stopped and played on the way to school. 10. Winter's cold frost and the northern blasts have come. 11. The little wren built its nest and reared its brood under the porch. 12. Butchers slaughter cattle and sheep, and carry their flesh to market to sell.

THE KINDS OF SENTENCES.

A sentence which can not be separated into two or more sentences is called a *Simple Sentence*.

Thus, "He will be loved," "He is good," and "He and I are loved," are simple sentences.

When one sentence or more than one are joined to another to explain it, or to change or complete its meaning, the sentences taken together form what is called a *Complex Sentence*.

The parts of a complex sentence are connected by the conjunctions *although, because, for, if, that, unless, until, when*, or by some similar conjunction.

Thus, "He will be loved, *because he is good*," and "I will come *when you call me*," are complex sentences.

Sentences whose parts are connected by *who, whose, whom, which, what*, or the like, are also complex sentences.

"Boys *who are honest*, will be trusted," is a complex sentence.

When two or more simple or complex sentences are connected by one conjunction or more, they are taken together, and form what is called a *Compound Sentence*.

The parts of a compound sentence are connected by the

conjunctions *also, and, but, or, nor,* or by some similar conjunction.

Thus, "He is good, *and* he will be loved," and "I was young, *but* now I am old," are compound sentences.

EXERCISE I.—Repeat the conjunctions which may be used to connect the parts or sentences which form a complex sentence.

Repeat the other words which may connect the parts of a complex sentence.

Repeat the conjunctions which may be used to connect the parts of a compound sentence.

Are two or more sentences united to form a simple sentence?

Are two or more sentences united to form a complex sentence?

What kinds of sentences may be united to form a compound sentence? How?

EXERCISE II.—Mention which of the following sentences are *simple,* which are *complex,* and which are *compound:—*

1. I love you. 2. John and I love you. 3. I love you, and you know it. 4. I love you, for you have done me good. 5. Has your brother a pair of nice silk gloves? 6. A little worm spun the silk of which they are made. 7. The morning sun proclaims that God is ever good. 8. If they did not have any sun, the grass and the trees could not grow. 9. I have been sick, but I am very well now. 10. Charles has not been very successful, yet he is not discouraged. 11. The snow was nearly two feet deep, for the storm had lasted through two days. 12. I am sorry because I laughed.

13. William has a pair of new skates, which his uncle George gave him for a Christmas present. 14. These flowers make a very pretty nosegay, but there is no moss-rose among them. 15. The day was warm, and the swing was put up under the shade of the trees. 16. Boys do not know what they can do until they try. 17. Martha had a large gray cat, which she prized very much, for the cat was a good mouser. 18. Snow and ice remain in Greenland all the year. 19. The little boys were not cold, for the hard work had kept them warm. 20. David's father and mother hoped that when spring came he would become better; but no, he became worse. 21. The farmer can not reap and mow if he does not plow and sow. 22. The wages of sin is death. 23. The worst enemy is sin, and the worst evil is the anger of God.

EXERCISE III.—Mention the *subjects* and the *predicates,* also the *subject-nominatives* and the *predicate-verbs,* contained in the preceding sentences.

Mention also, so far as you can, to what class each word belongs.

AN

ELEMENTARY GRAMMAR

OF THE

ENGLISH LANGUAGE.

GRAMMAR is the science which treats of the correct use of language.

Science is the principles of any branch of knowledge arranged according to system or in regular order.

Language is the means by which human beings express their thoughts in words. Language is either *spoken* or *written*.

ENGLISH GRAMMAR is the science which treats of the correct use of the English language, both in speaking and in writing.

When we speak, we use words: when we write, we use words; and the words which we write may be printed.

Words therefore are both *spoken*, and *written* or *printed*.

To represent the elementary sounds, or the simplest sounds that we utter in speaking, written signs called *letters* are used.

Letters properly arranged form written *words*.

Words so arranged as to express complete sense, or to assert something, form *sentences*.

When we speak or write in the usual way, we speak or write what is called *prose*. There is another way of arranging words and sentences, called *poetry*, or *verse*. Hymns and songs are verse.

English Grammar is divided into *four parts*.

The four parts of Grammar are ORTHOGRAPHY, ETYMOLOGY, SYNTAX, and PROSODY.

Orthography treats of *Letters*, and teaches how to spell correctly.

Etymology treats of *Words*, teaches how to classify them, and shows their changes of form and meaning.

Syntax treats of *Sentences*, and teaches how to construct them from words.

Prosody treats of *Verse*, and teaches how to arrange words according to the principles of Versification.

Part First.

ORTHOGRAPHY.

ORTHOGRAPHY treats of *Letters*, and teaches how to spell correctly.

Letters are particular marks or signs used to represent certain sounds of the human voice.

THE CLASSES OF LETTERS.

Letters are divided into two classes; Vowels and Consonants.

A **Vowel** is a letter which represents a simple, perfect sound; as, *a, e, o.*

That is, the sound made in uttering a vowel is a pure tone of the voice which is not interrupted in any way by the lips the teeth, or any other organ of speech.

C

A **Consonant** is a letter which represents a sound that can be perfectly made only with the aid of a vowel; as, *f, k, j.*

That is, a letter which is a consonant can not be fully pronounced or uttered unless the sound of a vowel is also heard.

Thus, *f* is pronounced as if spelled *e-f, ef; k* is pronounced as if spelled *k-a, ka.*

VOWELS.

A **Vowel** is a letter which represents a simple, perfect sound.

The vowels, or vowel letters, are *a, e, i, o, u,* and sometimes *w* and *y.*

W or *y* is a vowel when it ends a word or a syllable; when it is not followed in the same syllable by a vowel; or, when it is followed in the same syllable by a vowel not sounded; as, *boy, lowly; grown, sylph; style, owe.*

In every other position, *w* or *y* is a consonant.

EXERCISE.—Mention the *vowels* and the *consonants* in the following words, and give the reasons:—

Ice, welfare, terrier, white, awry, judgment, awkward, handkerchief, shrewd, advertise, gawky, lightning, symptom, gayety, Wednesday, wither, dulness, rhyme, sinewy, type, lizard.

DIPHTHONGS AND TRIPHTHONGS.

Two vowels may be used together to represent one sound.

When two vowels are used to represent one sound, they form what is called a *Diphthong;* as, *oa* in *load; oi* in *voice.*

There are two kinds of diphthongs; Proper and Improper.

A **Proper Diphthong** is one in which both vowels are sounded; as, *ou* in *mouse; oy* in *joyful.* There are four proper diphthongs; *oi, ou, oy,* and *ow.*

An **Improper Diphthong** is one in which but one of the vowels is sounded; as, *ea* in *beat; eu* in *neuter.*

Three vowels may be used together to represent one sound.

When three vowels are used to represent one sound, they form what is called a *Triphthong;* as, *eau* in *beauty; iew* in *view.*

There are two kinds of triphthongs; Proper and Improper.

A **Proper Triphthong** is one in which all three vowels are sounded; as, *uoy* in *buoy.*

An **Improper Triphthong** is one in which but one or two of the vowels are sounded; as, *eye, ieu* in *lieu.* The principal improper triphthongs are, *ieu, eau, iew.*

The consonant *q* is always followed by *u;* when so placed, *u* is never considered as a part of a diphthong or of a triphthong.

EXERCISE.—Mention the *proper* and the *improper diphthongs* and *triphthongs* in the following words, and give the reasons:—

August, creature, pigeon, pioneer, nutritious, good, beauteous, rouse, quoit, eight, said, niece, prairie, sewer, nauseous, loathe, portmanteau, quotient, pointer, bazaar, league, views.

CONSONANTS.

A **Consonant** is a letter which represents a sound that can be perfectly made only with the aid of a vowel.

The consonants are divided into two classes; Semi-vowels and Mutes.

Semi-vowels are letters which can be imperfectly sounded without the aid of a vowel; as, *c, j, v, y.*

They are *c* soft, *f, g* soft, *h, j, l, m, n, r, s, v, w, x, y,* and *z.*

C has its soft sound (the sound of *s*) before *e, i,* and *y;* before other letters it has the sound of *k.*

G has its soft sound (the sound of *j*) before *e, i,* and *y·* there are, however, some exceptions.

Four of the semi-vowels, *l, m, n,* and *r,* are called *liquids,* on account of their smooth and flowing sound.

Mutes are letters which can not be sounded without the aid of a vowel; as, *p, q, t, k.*

They are *b, c* hard, *d, g* hard, *k, p, q,* and *t.*

SYLLABLES.

A **Syllable** is a letter, or a number of letters, which when uttered, form one unbroken sound; as, *far, a-far, com-mence.*

A syllable may be either a word or a part of a word; if written, it always contains a vowel; if spoken, a vowel sound.

WORDS.

A **Written Word** is a letter, or a number of letters properly combined, used as the *sign* of some idea; as, *I, day, army.*

A **Spoken Word** is a sound, or a number of sounds combined, used to express some idea.

Words are named according to the number of syllables which they contain.

A word which contains one syllable is called a **Monosyllable**; as, *truth:* one which contains two syllables is called a **Dissyllable**; as, *truthful:* one which contains three syllables is called a **Trisyllable**; as, *untruthful:* one which contains more than three syllables is called a **Polysyllable**; as, *untruthfulness, incomprehensible.*

SPELLING.

Spelling is the art of combining letters properly, so as to form syllables and words.

The art of spelling is best learned from spelling-books and dictionaries, and from observation in reading.

THE PRINCIPAL RULES OF SPELLING.

THE DOUBLING OF THE FINAL CONSONANT.—1. The final consonant of a monosyllable or of a word accented on the last syllable, ending with a single consonant preceded by a single vowel, is doubled on receiving a suffix beginning with a vowel; as, *hot, hotter; occur, occurring; transfer, transferring.*

2. The final consonant is not doubled, if it is not preceded by a single vowel, if it is preceded by one or more consonants, or if the accent is not on the last syllable; as, *toil, toiling; sound, sounded; differ, different.*

WORDS ENDING WITH SILENT *E.*—1. In words ending with silent *e*, *e* is generally omitted on receiving a suffix beginning with a vowel; as, *move, movable; love, loved; able, abler.*

In words ending with *ce* or *ge*, *e* is retained before terminations beginning with *a*, *o*, or *u*, in order to preserve the soft sounds of *c* and *g*; as, *trace, traceable; courage, courageous.*

In words ending with *ie*, *e* is omitted and *i* changed into *y* before the termination *ing*, in order to prevent the doubling of *i*; as, *tie, tying; belie, belying.*

E is retained in *dye, singe, springe, swinge, tinge, hoe, shoe,* and *toe*, before the termination *ing*; as, *dye, dyeing; shoe, shoeing.*

2. In words ending with silent *e*, *e* is generally retained on receiving a suffix beginning with a consonant; as, *dire, direful; care, careless.*

The following words are exceptions:—*Abridgment, acknowledgment, argument, judgment, duly, truly, awful, nursling, wisdom, wholly.*

WORDS ENDING WITH *Y.*—1. In words ending with *y* immediately preceded by a consonant, *y* is changed into *i* on receiving one or more suffixed letters or syllables; as, *try, tries; lively, liveliest.*

Y is not changed into *i* before the termination *ing;* as, *dry, drying; rely, relying.*

2. In words ending with *y* immediately preceded by a vowel, *y* is retained on receiving one or more suffixed letters or syllables; as, *money, moneys; joy, joyful; pay, payable.*

Paid from *pay, laid* from *lay, said* and *saith* from *say, staid* from *stay,* and *daily* from *day,* are exceptions.

EXERCISE.—Apply the rule for forming each of the following words:—

MODEL 1.—Suffix *ed* to *tap.*

Tapped.—"Tap" is a monosyllable ending with a single consonant preceded by a single vowel; therefore the final consonant is doubled on receiving the suffix *ed,* which begins with a vowel; according to the Rule, "The final consonant of a monosyllable, etc."

2.—Suffix *es* to *try.*

Tries.—"Try" is a word ending with *y* immediately preceded by a consonant; therefore *y* is changed into *i* on receiving the suffixed letters *es;* according to the Rule, "In words ending with *y* immediately preceded by a consonant, etc."

3.—Suffix *ly* to *due.*

Duly.—"Due" is a word ending with silent *e;* therefore *e* should be retained on receiving the suffix *ly,* beginning with a consonant; but it is dropped, being an exception to the Rule, "In words ending with silent *e, e* is generally retained on receiving a suffix beginning with a consonant."

Suffix *ed* to pen, rob, beg, slip, harp, call, hate, remove, dye, care, defy, delay, say;—*er* to gay, employ, lovely, easy, lodge, shoe, begin, labor;—*ing* to hum, cool, scratch, refer, offer, sing, please, become, belie, singe, falsify, satisfy, destroy, display, convey.

Suffix *s* or *es,* as may be required, to prepare, apply, buoy, annoy, occupy, survey, notify, comply, espy, stray;—*ly* to love, intense, true, happy, funny, whole, late, strange;—*est* to admire, supply, enjoy, differ, forgive, forget, busy, tardy, ugly, waylay.

Part Second.

ETYMOLOGY.

ETYMOLOGY treats of *Words*, teaches how to classify them, and shows their changes of form and meaning.

THE CLASSES OF WORDS.

Words are divided into nine classes, called Parts of Speech.

The **Parts of Speech** are the NOUN, the PRONOUN, the ARTICLE, the ADJECTIVE, the VERB, the ADVERB, the PREPOSITION, the CONJUNCTION, and the INTERJECTION.

THE DEFINITIONS OF THE PARTS OF SPEECH.

A **Noun** is a word used as the name of any thing; as, *Washington, country, beauty, soul.*

A **Pronoun** is a word used in place of a noun; as, "Henry loves *his* books; *he* studies *his* lessons well."

An **Article** is the word *the,* or *a* or *an,* which is used before a noun to limit its meaning; as, *The* star; *a* house; *an* insect.

An **Adjective** is a word used to describe or limit a noun or a pronoun; as, A *sweet* apple; *many* books; "He is *good.*"

A **Verb** is a word used to assert action, being, or

state; as, "James *runs*."—"He *does* something." "I *am* here."—"The child *sleeps*."

An **Adverb** is a word used to qualify the meaning of a verb, an adjective, or another adverb; as, "He is *very* industrious, and advances *rapidly* in his studies."

A **Preposition** is a word used before a noun or a pronoun to show its relation to some preceding word; as, "The boy went *with* his father *to* the library."

A **Conjunction** is a word used to connect the words, the parts of a sentence, or the sentences, between which it is placed; as, "He is patient *and* happy, *because* he is a Christian."

An **Interjection** is a word used in exclamation, to express some emotion of the mind; as, *Ah! Alas!*

EXERCISE.—Tell to which *part of speech* each word in the following sentences belongs, and give the reason:—

MODEL.—"Oh! how the bright sun pours its beams over hill and vale!"

Oh.—"Oh" is an interjection, because it is a word used merely as an exclamation:—"An Interjection is a word used in exclamation, to express some emotion of the mind."

How.—"How" is an adverb, because it is a word used to qualify the meaning of the verb *pours:*—"An Adverb is a word used to qualify a verb, an adjective, or another adverb."

The.—"The" is an article, because it is a word used before the noun *sun* to limit its meaning:—"An Article is the word *the*, or *a* or *an*, which is placed before a noun to limit its meaning."

Bright.—"Bright" is an adjective, because it is a word used to describe the noun *sun:*—"An Adjective is a word used to describe or limit a noun or a pronoun."

Sun.—"Sun" is a noun, because it is a word used as a name:—"A Noun is a word used as the name of any thing."

Pours.—"Pours" is a verb, because it is a word used to assert action of *sun:*—"A Verb is a word used to assert action, being, or state."

Its.—"It" is a pronoun, because it is a word used in place of the noun *sun's:*—"A Pronoun is a word used in place of a noun."

Beams.—"Beams" is a noun, because it is a word used as a name:—"A Noun is a word used as the name of any thing."

Over.—"Over" is a preposition, because it is a word used before the nouns *hill* and *vale*, to show their relation to the verb *pours:*—"A Preposition is a word used before a noun or a pronoun to show its relation to some preceding word."

Hill.—"Hill" is a noun, because it is a word used as a name:—"A Noun is a word used as the name of any thing."

And.—"And" is a Conjunction, because it is a word used to connect the nouns *hill* and *vale:*—"A Conjunction is a word used to connect the words, the parts of a sentence, or the sentences, between which it is placed."

Vale.—"Vale" is a noun, because it is a word used as a name:—"A Noun is a word used as the name of any thing."

1. The earth is not flat; it is round. 2. Men can sail round the world in ships. 3. The day was hot; so we sat in the cool shade of the trees. 4. A beautiful picture hung in the window of a print-shop in State Street. 5. The morning was bright, and at an early hour the driver of the sleigh-stage was at the door. 6. Alas! how we miss the kind words and the gentle touch of our dear mother! 7. Robinson Crusoe spent many years on a lonely island. 8. Sir William Wallace was the son of noble parents; he was born in 1277. 9. Contentment is better than riches. 10. No man is truly great unless he is truly good.

11. Good advice is too often neglected. 12. Industry in brown clothes is better than idleness in splendid rags. 13. All the stars were pale and dim, because the full moon shone so brilliantly. 14. The dear old flag, with its broad stripes and bright stars, floated proudly in the breeze. 15. Mercy becomes a monarch better than his crown. 16. The thoughts of home brought bitter tears to the eyes of the little wanderer. 17. The bell rang, and they soon stopped their play and went to bed. 18. A small but clear stream of water trickled through the crevice, glistened along the thirsty sands for a moment, and then disappeared.

4*

NOUNS.

A **Noun** is a word used as the name of any thing; as, *James, Anna, boy, girl, river, truth.*

CLASSES OF NOUNS.

Nouns are divided into two general classes; Proper and Common.

A **Proper Noun** is a word used as the name of a particular object or collection of objects, to distinguish it from others of the same class; as, *John, Troy, Ohio, the Alps.*

The word *John* is used as the name of a *particular person*, to distinguish him from James and George and William, and all other men or boys.

A **Common Noun** is a word used as the name of any object or collection of objects of the same class; as, *man, city, river, mountains.*

The word *man* does not distinguish John, James, or Henry from any other man; it is a name *common to all men.*

A noun is called **Complex,** when it is formed of two or more words not united, used together as one name; as, *Dead Sea, Chief Justice Marshall, Duke of Wellington.*

A noun is called **Compound,** when it is formed of two or more words united, used as one name; as, *statesman, landlord, man-of-war.*

A **Collective Noun** is a word used as the name of a collection of beings or of things, regarded as a unit; as, *family, herd, class.*

EXERCISE I.—Tell to which *class* each of the following nouns belongs, and give the reason:—

Robert, Robinson Crusoe, islands, crowd, word, Thomas Jefferson, Thomas, month, April, state, New Hampshire, science, giant-killer, Prince of Wales, regiment, base-ball, navy, river, Astor Library, Penobscot, fractions, King Henry, cloud, board, grammar, pronoun, Iowa City, the Romans, Rome, legislature, the East Indies, johnny-jump-up, panther, printer, noise, senate, he-goat, the Prussians, molasses, strawberry, croquet, bookcase.

EXERCISE II.—Write five sentences, each containing a *common* noun;—five, each containing a *proper* noun;—five, each containing a *collective* noun;—five, each containing a *complex* noun;—and five, each containing a *compound* noun.

PROPERTIES OF NOUNS.

Property, in Grammar, means a peculiar quality belonging to any part of speech.

Nouns have four properties; Number, Person, Gender, and Case.

NUMBER.

Number is that property of a noun which denotes whether one object or collection of objects is meant, or more than one.

Nouns have two numbers; the Singular and the Plural.

The **Singular Number** denotes one object, or a collection of objects considered as a unit; as, *desk, bench, nation, flock.*

The **Plural Number** denotes more than one object or collection of objects; as, *desks, benches, nations.*

THE FORMATION OF THE PLURAL.

Nouns generally become plural by the suffixing of *s* to the singular; as, sing. *home,* plur. *homes; key, keys; rose, roses; clock, clocks; cameo, cameos.*

This rule always applies to nouns ending with *o, u,* or *y* immediately preceded by a vowel; as, *bay, bays; trio, trios; purlieu, purlieus.*

EXERCISES.

Nouns ending with *ch* (not sounded as *k*), *s*, *sh*, *x* or *z*. become plural by the suffixing of *es* to the singular; as, *bunch, bunches; gas, gases; sash, sashes; fox, foxes; waltz, waltzes.*

Nouns ending with *y* immediately preceded by a consonant, become plural by the change of *y* into *i* and the suffixing of *es*; as, *study, studies; army, armies.*

Some nouns ending with single *f* or *fe*, become plural by the change of *f* into *v* and the suffixing of *es*; as, *life, lives; thief, thieves.*

These nouns are *beef, calf, elf, half, leaf, loaf, self, sheaf, shelf, thief, wolf, knife, life, wife.*

Other nouns ending with single *f* or *fe*, become plural by the general rule; but *wharf* has two forms of the plural, *wharfs* and *wharves.*

Nouns ending with *ff*, become plural by the general rule; as, *muff, muffs;* but *staff,* meaning a cane, has *staves* for the plural; its compounds, however, become plural by the suffixing of *s* only; as, *flagstaffs, distaffs.*

Nouns ending with *o* preceded by a consonant, differ in the formation of the plural. Some become plural by the suffixing of *es*; as, *echo, echoes; hero, heroes;*—others by the suffixing of *s* only; as, *solo, solos; piano, pianos.*

The following nouns have irregular plurals:—

Sing.	Plur.	Sing.	Plur.	Sing.	Plur.
Man,	men.	Foot,	feet.	Goose,	geese.
Child,	children.	Tooth,	teeth.	Louse,	lice.
Woman,	women.	Ox,	oxen.	Mouse,	mice.

REMARKS.

Such nouns as *goodness, gold, geometry,* and *wisdom,* are always in the singular.

Such nouns as *ashes, cattle, drugs, manners, morals, oats, scissors, thanks,* and *victuals,* are plural only.

Such nouns as *deer, fish, sheep,* and *trout,* have the same form in the plural as in the singular.

EXERCISES.

EXERCISE I.—Apply the rule for forming the plural of each of the following nouns:—

MODEL.—*Lady*.—The plural of *lady* is *ladies*.

"Lady" is a noun ending with *y* immediately preceded by the consonant *d;* therefore the plural is formed by the change of *y* into *i* and the suffixing of *es*, according to the Rule, "Nouns ending with *y* immediately preceded by a consonant, become plural by the change of *y* into *i* and the suffixing of *es*."

Mass, sky, piano, body, ditch, wolf, chintz, knife, trio, box, wish, calf, scarf, watch, muff, echo, miss, home, pulley, hoof, colony, delay, solo, folly, turkey, grief, scratch, buoy, block, gash, loss, coach, sheaf, life, wharf, hero, governess, peach, alley, strife, studio.

EXERCISE II.—Spell the singular of each of the following nouns:—

Beaus, wives, countesses, fathers, geese, horses, lasses, ladies, misses, witches, men, cargoes, priests, potatoes, mottoes, paths, cameos, tipstaffs, wharves, fifes, beeves, bunches, cabbages, mice, baronesses, mementos, grottos, teeth.

EXERCISE III.—Name each *noun* in the following sentences, the *class* to which it belongs, and its *number*, and give the reasons:—

MODEL.—" How high the birds soar!"

Birds.—"Birds" is a noun, because it is a word used as a name; it is a common noun, because it is a word used as the name of any object or collection of objects of the same class; it is in the plural number, because it denotes more than one object.

1. There are often many ways of doing the same thing. 2. Mild words disarm anger. 3. The army passed over the river on pontoon bridges. 4. Benjamin West made his first drawings with charcoal. 5. Vast herds of buffaloes once roamed over the fertile prairies of Illinois. 6. The men obeyed his command, and, before it was day, marched into the town. 7. The name of Robert Bruce is known to many a school-boy. 8. The artist spent many months at his easel. 9. Early in the morning the fleet left the harbor of New York. 10. In the neighborhood was a wild stream, which wound among the hills for many miles.

EXERCISE IV.—Write ten sentences, each containing one noun or more in the singular number:—ten, each containing one noun or more in the plural.

PERSON.

Person is that property of a noun which distinguishes the speaker or writer, the person or thing addressed, and the person or thing mentioned.

Nouns have three persons; the First, the Second, and the Third.

The **First Person** is that which denotes the speaker or writer; as, "I, *James*, will go."

The **Second Person** is that which denotes the person or thing addressed; as, "*James* will you go?"

The **Third Person** is that which denotes the person or thing mentioned; as, "*James* will go."—"*Leaves* fall."

Nouns are rarely used in the first person: in the majority of sentences nouns are in the third person.

EXERCISE I.—Tell to which *class* each *noun* in the following sentences belongs; tell its *number* and its *person*, and give the reasons:—

MODEL.—"Frank, come to me presently."

Frank.—"Frank" is a noun, because it is a word used as a name; it is a proper noun, because it is a word used as the name of a particular object to distinguish it from others of the same class; it is in the singular number, because it denotes but one object; it is in the second person, because it denotes the person addressed.

1. The trees dipped their branches into the stream. 2. Little hands gathered the violets and the honeysuckles. 3. Oh! mother, to-morrow will be the first of May. 4. Quakers, or Friends, will not take an oath. 5. I, James, do promise to perform all of my duties faithfully. 6. What did your friend say, Charles, when you delivered the note? 7. At an early hour the group of children were ready to start. 8. Boys, let me entreat you to avoid falsehood and profanity. 9. The father and his sons were walking through the green fields. 10. Scholars, how many of you try to please your teacher by obeying her in all things?

EXERCISE II.—Write five sentences, each containing a noun in the first person;—five, each containing a noun in the second person;—five, each containing one noun or more in the third person.

GENDER.

Gender is that property of nouns which distinguishes them in regard to sex.

In grammar, the term *gender* is applied to *words* used as the names of objects; just as in nature the term *sex* is applied to those *objects* themselves.

Nouns have three genders; the Masculine, the Feminine, and the Neuter.

The **Masculine Gender** is that which denotes beings of the male sex; as, *father, king, stag.*

The **Feminine Gender** is that which denotes beings of the female sex; as, *mother, queen, hind.*

The **Neuter Gender** is that which denotes objects that are without sex; as, *table, book, mountain, wisdom.*

Some nouns, such as *parent, child, friend,* denote beings that may be either male or female; they are therefore either of the masculine or of the feminine gender.

In the following list, the masculine and the feminine gender are distinguished by the use of different words:—

Masculine.	*Feminine.*	*Masculine.*	*Feminine.*
Bachelor,	maid.	Husband,	wife.
Beau,	belle.	King,	queen.
Boy,	girl.	Lad,	lass.
Brother,	sister.	Lord,	lady.
Buck,	doe.	Male,	female.
Bull,	cow.	Master,	miss, mistress.
Cock,	hen.	Nephew,	niece.
Drake,	duck.	Papa,	mamma.
Earl,	countess.	Ram,	ewe.
Father,	mother.	Sir,	madam.
Friar, monk,	nun.	Son,	daughter.
Gander,	goose.	Stag,	hind.
Hart,	roe.	Uncle,	aunt.
Horse,	mare.	Wizard,	witch.

Many nouns of the feminine gender are formed from the masculine by suffixing *ess, ine,* etc.; as, masc. *poet,* fem. *poetess; hero, heroine; don, donna;* etc.

EXERCISE I.—Mention each *noun* in the following sentences, and the *class* to which it belongs; also its *number, person,* and *gender,* and give the reasons:—

MODEL.—" How sweet the flowers smell!"

Flowers.—"Flowers" is a noun, because it is a word used as a name; it is a common noun, because it is used as the name of any object of the same class; it is in the plural number, because it denotes more than one object; it is in the third person, because it denotes the things mentioned; it is of the neuter gender, because it denotes objects that are without sex.

1. The gardener gathered several flowers for him. 2. The horse with the boy upon his back walked slowly up the hill. 3. Father, where do the bees find the wax to make their cells? 4. The water flowed slowly between the banks. 5. Herbert sat by the small fire at home, with his head resting upon his hands. 6. Why, man, what ails you? you look as pale as a sheet. 7. A painter could not have wished for a better model. 8. When Helen reached the school, all the pupils had taken their seats. 9. The clouds moved slowly across the blue vault of heaven. 10. A bold heart and a strong arm will carry us through difficulties.

EXERCISE II.—Write ten sentences, each containing one noun or more in the masculine gender;—ten, each containing one or more in the feminine gender;- -ten, each containing one or more in the neuter gender.

CASE.

Case is that property of nouns which distinguishes their relations to other words.

Nouns have three cases; the Nominative, the Possessive, and the Objective.

The **Nominative Case** is that which usually denotes the subject of a verb; as, "The *boy* reads."

The *subject* of a *verb* is that of which something is either said or asserted.

THE DECLENSION OF NOUNS. 51

The **Possessive Case** is that which usually denotes possession or origin; as, The *boy's* book; *Milton's* poems.

The **Objective Case** is that which usually denotes the object of a verb, or of a preposition; as, "The boy *struck* his *sister*."—"The apple is sweet *to* the *taste*."

The *object* of a *verb* is that upon which the action asserted by the verb is exerted. The *object* of a *preposition* is the object of the relation shown by the preposition.

THE FORMS OF THE CASES.

The nominative case and the objective are alike in form. They are distinguished from each other by their relations to other words.

The possessive case may always be known by its form.

The possessive case in the singular number is usually formed by suffixing the apostrophe and *s* ('*s*) to the nominative singular; as, nom. *day*, poss. *day's*.

The possessive case in the plural number is formed by suffixing the apostrophe only to the nominative plural when the nominative plural ends with *s*, and by suffixing both the apostrophe and *s* when the nominative plural does not end with *s*.

Thus, nom. *days*, poss. *days'*; nom. *men*, poss. *men's*.

THE DECLENSION OF NOUNS.

The **Declension** of nouns is the regular arrangement of their numbers and cases.

EXAMPLES OF DECLENSION.
Singular.

Nom.	Money,	Ox,	Sky,	James,	Wife,	Glass,
Poss.	money's,	ox's,	sky's,	James's,	wife's,	glass's,
Obj.	money;	ox;	sky;	James;	wife;	glass;

Plural.

Nom.	moneys,	oxen,	skies,	Jameses,	wives,	glasses,
Poss.	moneys',	oxen's,	skies',	Jameses',	wives',	glasses',
Obj.	moneys.	oxen.	skies.	Jameses.	wives.	glasses.

EXERCISE.—*Decline* each of the following nouns:—

Man, yard, lady, peach, bay, goose, mouse, ladle, knife, miss, Charles, year, box, army, sash, study, thief, muff, fife, buffalo, child, page, actor, block, folio, waltz, brush, body loaf, staff (a stick), chimney, salesman.

SUBJECT AND OBJECT.

The *subject* of a verb may be known by asking the question formed by placing *who* or *what* before the verb; the answer to the question is the subject.

Thus, take the sentence, "John studies his lesson." *Who* studies? The answer is, *John*. Hence *John* is the subject of the verb *studies*, and therefore is in the *nominative case*.

The *object* of a verb or of a preposition may be known by asking the question formed by placing *whom* or *what* after the verb or the preposition: the answer to the question will be the object.

Thus, "Henry studies grammar." Studies *what?* *Grammar*. Grammar is the object of the action asserted or expressed by the verb *studies*, and therefore is in the *objective case*.

"He spoke to his teacher." To *whom?* To *teacher*. Hence *teacher* is the object of the relation shown by the preposition *to*, and therefore is in the *objective case*.

EXERCISE I.—Name the nouns in the *nominative*, and those in the *objective* case in the following sentences, and give the reasons:—

1. The bad boy struck the dog. 2. The deer ran to the hills. 3. The men cut down the trees. 4. The stars shone brightly in the qu et sky. 5. Only a cruel person will do harm to others. 6. A tall, kind-looking man stepped up to the stranger. 7. Tall maples crowned the summit of the hill. 8. The day for the commencement arrived, and they prepared to attend. 9. The exercises were long and tiresome, and we were glad when they came to a close. 10. In 1814, the city of Washington was captured by a British army under General Ross.

EXERCISE II.—Write ten sentences, each containing one noun or more in the nominative case;—ten, each containing one or more in the possessive;—ten, each containing one or more in the objective.

PARSING.

To Parse means to tell to what parts of speech words belong, to name their properties and relations, and to give the rules which apply to them.

As the *rules* are given in *Syntax* only, they may be omitted at present in parsing.

In *parsing*, it is well to name (1) the word to be parsed; (2) the word or the words with which it is grammatically connected; and (3) its properties, relations, etc.

EXERCISE.—*Parse* each *noun* in the following sentences:—

MODEL.—"The boys found a bird's nest in the grove."

Boys.—Boys *found.*—"Boys" is a noun, "A Noun is a word used as the name of any thing";—a common noun, because it is used as the name of any collection of objects of the same class;—in the plural number, because it denotes more than one object;—in the third person, because it denotes the persons mentioned;—of the masculine gender, because it denotes beings of the male sex;—in the nominative case, because it is the subject of the verb *found*.

Bird's.—Bird's *nest.*—"Bird's" is a noun, "A Noun is a word, etc.";—a common noun, because it is used as the name of any object of the same class;—in the singular number, because it denotes one object;—in the third person, because it denotes the being mentioned;—of the masculine or the feminine gender, because it denotes a being of the male or of the female sex;—in the possessive case, because it denotes possession.

Nest.—*Found* nest.—"Nest" is a noun, "A Noun is a word, etc.";—a common noun, because it is used as the name of any object of the same class;—in the singular number, because it denotes one object;—in the third person, because it denotes the thing mentioned;—of the neuter gender, because it denotes an object without sex;—in the objective case, because it is the object of the action asserted or expressed by the verb *found*.

Grove.—In grove.—"Grove" is a noun, "A Noun is a word, etc.";—a common noun, because it is used as the name of any object of the same class;—in the singular number, because it denotes one object;—in the third person, because it denotes the thing mentioned;—of the neuter gender, because it denotes an object without sex;—in the objective case, because it is the object of the relation shown by the preposition *in*.

1. Virginia was settled at Jamestown. 2. The wreck was washed upon the shore. 3. The streams overflowed their banks. 4. A gloomy house stood by the roadside. 5. Bleak winds whistled through the pines around the cabin. 6. The broad flakes of snow soon hid the ground from view. 7. An ice-boat was rigged, and the wind blew the party across the pond. 8. Travelers suffer from heat and thirst as they cross the desert. 9. The Indians' hunting grounds are now cultivated. 10. The lion's roar echoed far and wide through the forest. 11. The moments of youth are more precious than rubies are. 12. Grace Darling aided her father in saving the lives of many shipwrecked persons. 13. The Falls of St. Anthony are in the Mississippi River. 14. The council-fires of the red men then blazed in the forests which have since bowed before the axe of the settler. 15. The old man's advice was rejected by the thoughtless youth.

PRONOUNS.

A Pronoun is a word used in place of a noun; as, "Thomas deserves praise, for *he* has recited *his* lessons well."

In this sentence the word *he* is used in place of the noun *Thomas*, and *his* in place of the noun *Thomas's;* the words *he* and *his* are therefore called *pronouns*,—a word which means "for nouns."

A pronoun is used to avoid an unpleasant repetition of a noun.

The noun for which a pronoun is used is called the *antecedent* of the pronoun, because it generally *precedes* the pronoun, and the latter is said to *represent* its antecedent.

In the sentence, "Thomas has recited his lessons," the noun *Thomas* is the *antecedent* of the pronoun *his*, and the pronoun *represents* its antecedent *Thomas*.

PROPERTIES OF PRONOUNS.

As pronouns represent nouns, they have *number, person, gender,* and *case,* as nouns have. They have also *declension*.

The number, the person, and the gender of a pronoun are always the same as those of the noun which it represents, but the *case* may be different.

CLASSES OF PRONOUNS.

Pronouns are divided into three classes; Personal, Relative, and Interrogative.

PERSONAL PRONOUNS.

A **Personal Pronoun** is one that shows by its form the *person* of the noun which it represents.

Personal pronouns are Simple or Compound.

The **Simple Personal Pronouns** are *I, thou, he, she,* and *it,* and their variations in the singular and in the plural.

I is in the first person, and of the masculine or of the feminine gender.

Thou is in the second person, masculine or feminine gender.

He is in the third person, masculine gender: *she* is in the third person, feminine gender: *it* is in the third person, neuter gender.

THE DECLENSION OF THE SIMPLE PERSONAL PRONOUNS.

Singular.

	First Person. Masc. or Fem.	Second Person. Masc. or Fem.	Third Person. Masc.	Fem.	Neut.
Nom.	I,	Thou,	He,	She,	It,
Poss.	my, *or* mine,	thy, *or* thine,	his,	her, *or* hers,	its,
Obj.	me;	thee;	him;	her;	it;

Plural.

Nom.	we,	you, *or* ye,	they,	they,	they,
Poss.	our, *or* ours,	your, *or* yours,	their, *or* theirs,	their, *or* theirs,	their, *or* theirs,
Obj.	us.	you.	them.	them.	them.

REMARKS.

In the possessive case, *my, thy, her, our, your, their*, are used when the noun denoting the thing possessed is mentioned, and *mine, thine, hers, ours, yours, theirs*, when it is omitted; as, "This work is *mine*."—"This is *my* work."

The apostrophe (') should never be used in writing the following forms of pronouns in the possessive case: *hers, its, ours, yours, theirs;* as, "It is *yours*," not *your's*.

In the singular number, second person, the plural forms *you, your,* and *yours,* are commonly used, though but one individual is addressed; as, "John, have *you* studied *your* lesson?"

The form *thou* is used in prayers to God, in solemn language, and in poetry.

COMPOUND PERSONAL PRONOUNS.

Compound Personal Pronouns are formed by subjoining in the singular the word *self* to the simple personal pronouns *my, thy, him, her,* and *it;* and in the plural, the word *selves* to *our, your,* and *them.*

The Compound Personal Pronouns are *myself, thyself, himself, herself,* and *itself,* and their plural forms *ourselves, yourselves,* and *themselves.*

THE DECLENSION OF THE COMPOUND PERSONAL PRONOUNS.

Singular.

	First Person. *Masc. or Fem.*	*Second Person.* *Masc. or Fem.*	*Third Person.*		
			Masculine.	*Feminine.*	*Neuter.*
Nom.	Myself,	Thyself,	Himself,	Herself,	Itself.
Poss.	———	———	———	———	———
Obj.	myself;	thyself;	himself;	herself;	itself;

Plural.

Nom. ourselves, yourselves, themselves, themselves, themselves,
Poss. ——— ——— ——— ——— ———
Obj. ourselves. yourselves. themselves. themselves. themselves.

The compound personal pronouns have no form for the possessive case, either in the singular or in the plural.

EXERCISE I.—Tell the *number*, the *person*, the *gender*, and the *case* of each of the following pronouns:—

Ours, thee, himself, it, I, you, herself, he, we, thyself, they, myself, your, thine, ourselves, thou, us, themselves, my, its, itself, mine, ours.

EXERCISE II.—Write six sentences, containing different pronouns in the first person;—six, containing different pronouns in the second person;—twelve, containing different pronouns in the third person.

EXERCISE III.—Parse the *personal pronouns* in the following sentences:—

MODEL.—"The boy lost his books and could not find them."

His.—(*Boy*) his *books.*—"*His*" is a personal pronoun, "A Personal Pronoun is one, etc.";—it is in the singular number, third person, and of the masculine gender, because the noun *boy*, which it represents, is;—in the possessive case, because it denotes possession.

Them.—*Could find* them (*books*).—"*Them*" is a personal pronoun, "A Personal Pronoun is one, etc.";—it is in the plural number, third person, and of the neuter gender, because the noun *books*, which it represents, is;—in the objective case, because it is the object of the action expressed by the verb *could find*.

1. Make the best of life, for it is short. 2. Indians are treacherous in their character. 3. James struck his brother with his fist. 4. There goes Mary with her satchel of books. 5. Harry has a little carriage, and he often rides in it. 6. The old hen calls her young ones when she finds

a worm for them. 7. Pet rabbits are fond of play, and they often chase each other for hours at a time. 8. A scorner seeketh wisdom, and findeth it not. 9. The snow spreads its white sheet over the whole country. 10. Martha fancied herself slighted. 11. Come, we must now commence our studies. 12. The soldiers threw themselves upon the ground, and the balls passed over their heads.

EXERCISE IV.—Parse also the nouns in the preceding sentences.

RELATIVE PRONOUNS.

A Relative Pronoun is one which relates directly to some preceding noun or pronoun; as, "*Thomas, who* came late, was not admitted."—"*He who* wins, may laugh."

The noun or the pronoun to which a relative pronoun relates is called its *antecedent*, because it is generally *placed before* the relative.

Relative Pronouns have no separate forms to distinguish the different persons, as the personal pronouns have. The person is determined by the antecedent, with which a relative always agrees in number, person, and gender.

Relative pronouns are of two kinds; Simple and Compound.

SIMPLE RELATIVES.

The Simple Relative Pronouns are *who, which, what,* and *that.*

THE DECLENSION OF THE SIMPLE RELATIVES.

Singular.

Nom.	Who,	Which,	What,	That,
Poss.	whose,	whose,	——	——
Obj.	whom;	which;	what;	that;

Plural.

Nom.	who,	which,	what,	that,
Poss.	whose,	whose,	——	——
Obj.	whom.	which.	what.	that.

REMARKS.

Who is used in referring to persons; as, "Elizabeth, *who* was Queen of England, died in 1603."

Which is used in referring to inferior animals and to things without life; as, "The deer *which* was killed."—"The flower *which* was plucked."

What is used in referring to things only. It is always of the neuter gender.

What is equivalent to *the thing which* (or *that which*) in the singular, and to *the things which* (or *those which*) in the plural.

Thus, "He obtained *what* he wanted," in the singular means, "He obtained *the thing which* he wanted;" and in the plural, "He obtained *the things which* he wanted."

That is sometimes used in referring to persons, animals, or things; as, "The same person *that* I knew."—"The last book *that* was bought."

COMPOUND RELATIVES.

The Compound Relative Pronouns are formed by subjoining the word *ever* or *soever* to the simple relatives *who*, *which*, and *what*.

The Compound Relatives are *whoever*, *whosoever*, *whichever*, *whichsoever*, *whatever*, and *whatsoever*.

THE DECLENSION OF THE COMPOUND RELATIVES.
Singular and Plural.

Nominative.	Possessive.	Objective.
Whoever,	whosever,	whomever,
Whosoever,	whosesoever,	whomsoever.
Whichever,	——	whichever.
Whichsoever,	——	whichsoever.
Whatever,	——	whatever.
Whatsoever,	——	whatsoever.

A compound relative includes, in meaning, an antecedent and a simple relative. *Whoever* and *whosoever* mean *any one who; whichever* and *whichsoever* mean *any one which; whatever* and *whatsoever* mean *any thing which,* or *all things which.*

INTERROGATIVE PRONOUNS.

An **Interrogative Pronoun** is one used to ask a question; as, "*Who* discovered America?"—"*Whose* book have you?"—"*Whom* did you meet?"

The Interrogatives are *who*, *which*, and *what*. They are declined like the simple relatives.

Who is used in asking about persons; as, "*Who* banished Napoleon?"—"*Who* invented gunpowder?"

Which and *what* are used in asking about persons, animals, or things; as, "*Which* of the men escaped?"—"*Which* of the horses won the race?"—"*What* is he? A *poet*."

An interrogative pronoun has no antecedent; but refers to some word in the answer, called the *subsequent*, with which it agrees in number, person, and gender; as, "*Who* invented the telegraph? *Morse*."

EXERCISE I.—Write ten sentences, containing simple relative pronouns;—ten, containing compound relative pronouns;—ten, containing interrogatives.

EXERCISE II.—Parse the *relative* and the *interrogative pronouns* in the following sentences:—

MODELS.—1. "Herbert, who skated well, glided swiftly over the ice."

Who.—(*Herbert*) who *skated*.—"Who" is a relative pronoun, "A Relative Pronoun is one, etc."; it is in the singular number, third person, and of the masc. gender, because its antecedent *Herbert*, to which it relates, is;—in the nom. case, because it is the subject of the verb *skated*.

2. "Whose flower is this? Mary's."

Whose.—(*Mary's*) whose *flower*.—"Whose" is an interrogative pronoun, "An Interrogative Pronoun is, etc."; it is in the sing. number, third person, and of the fem. gender, because its subsequent (*Mary's*) is, with which it agrees;—in the poss. case, because it denotes possession.

1. Remember the good advice which is given to you. 2. All the money that was given to him was lost. 3. The robbers who stopped him, threatened to take his life. 4. Who is your neighbor? Every man. 5. The wren, which perched on the branch, poured forth his melody 6. The panther, which had been crouching, now prepared for a spring. 7. Two young men, who were friends, set out to travel in distant lands

8. Wyoming Valley, which is in Pennsylvania, is noted for its beauty. 9. The gardener, whose flowers we admired, plucked a few for us. 10. Great masses, which carry all before them, rush down the mountain-side. 11. To whom was the message sent? To his brother. 12. He who despises little things, will never attain to great things.

EXERCISE III.—Parse the nouns and the personal pronouns in the preceding sentences.

ARTICLES.

An Article is the word *the*, or *a* or *an*, which is used before a noun to limit its meaning; as, "*The* sun, *the* earth; *an* eagle, *a* man.

There are two articles; *The*, and *A* or *An*.

The is called the Definite Article, because it shows that some object or collection of objects is referred to in a *definite* manner; as, *The* army, *the* cities.

In the expression, "the army," *the* shows that a *particular* army is meant; it limits the idea expressed by the word *army* to some particular object.

A is called the Indefinite Article, because it shows that an object is referred to in an *indefinite* manner; as, *A* battle, *an* army, *a* book.

In the expression, "a battle," *a* shows that *no particular* battle is meant; it does not limit the idea expressed by the word *battle* to any particular battle.

A and *an* are the same in meaning, but they differ in use.

An is used before words which, when uttered, begin with a vowel sound; as, *An* acorn, *an* honor.

A is used before words which, when uttered, begin with a consonant sound; as, *A* watch, *a* unit, *a* youth.

EXERCISE I.—Tell before which of the following words *a* should be used, and before which *an* should be used, and give the reasons:—

Indian, oyster, onion, union, hundred, humble, youth, order, use, icicle, history, European, uncle, idea, age, hero, height, truth, eye, humane, eagle, dream.

EXERCISE II.—Write ten sentences, each containing the indefinite article *a* or *an* properly used.

EXERCISE III.—Parse the *articles* in the following sentences:—

MODEL.—"The crow built its nest in a high tree."

The.—The *crow.*—"The" is an article, "An Article is the word, etc.";
it is the definite article, because it refers to the noun *crow* in a definite or particular manner.

A.—A *tree.*—"A" is an article, "An Article is the word, etc.";—it is the indefinite article, because it refers to the noun *tree* in an indefinite manner.

1. The scholars are at play on the lawn. 2. An intemperate person leads an unhappy life. 3. A large vessel struck upon the rocks. 4. A famine brought suffering upon the people. 5. An honest intention is good, but an honest act is better. 6. The page of his book was blotted. 7. The hunter shot a deer as it fed in an open plain.

EXERCISE IV.—Parse the nouns and the pronouns in the preceding sentences.

ADJECTIVES.

An **Adjective** is a word used to describe or limit a noun or a pronoun; as, *Ripe* apples; *three wise* men; *unhappy* me.

Thus, in the sentence, "Ripe apples fall," *ripe* denotes the *condition* of the apples that fall. The word *ripe* is therefore an *adjective* describing the noun *apples.*

In the sentence, "Three men came," *three* limits the *number* of men that came. The word *three* is therefore an *adjective* limiting the noun *men.*

CLASSES OF ADJECTIVES.

Adjectives may be divided into the following classes: Proper, Common, Numeral, and Pronominal.

A **Proper Adjective** is one derived from a proper noun; as, *American, English, Newtonian.*

A **Common Adjective** is one which describes or limits a noun or a pronoun, but which is not derived from a proper noun; as, *honest, numerous, perfect.*

A **Numeral Adjective** is one which denotes a definite number; as, *two, third, single.*

Numeral adjectives are of three kinds; Cardinal, Ordinal, and Multiplicative.

The **Cardinals** denote *how many;* as, *nine, ninety.*

The **Ordinals** denote *order;* as, *ninth, ninetieth.*

The **Multiplicatives** denote *how many fold;* as, *single, double* or *twofold, triple* or *threefold.*

REMARKS.

Adjectives, like nouns, may be *compound* in form; as, *Sweet-scented* clover; *home-made* bread; the *Anglo-Saxon* race.

Most numeral adjectives may be regarded as *complex* in form; as, *One hundred and nine* dollars; the *two hundred and tenth* page.

A noun becomes an adjective when it is used to describe another noun; as, *Croton* water, *gold* chain, *iron* castings.

Adjectives are sometimes used as nouns, and, as such, they have all the properties of nouns; as, "The *good* will be rewarded."—"We respect our *superiors.*"

EXERCISE I.—Write ten sentences, containing proper adjectives; —ten, containing common adjectives;—ten, containing numerals.

EXERCISE II.—Name the *adjectives* in the following sentences, tell to which *class* each belongs, and give the reasons:—

MODEL.—"The telegraph is an American invention."

American.—"American" is an adjective, because it describes the noun *invention;* it is a proper adjective, because it is derived from the proper noun *America.*

1. Four heavy wagons passed along the street. 2. The red squirrel is a blithe creature. 3. He leaps among the topmost branches of the great oak. 4. The brutal murderer had a low, narrow, and flat fore-

head. 5. The beautiful landscape was spread out like a bright picture before us. 6. The Indian chief glared at him with a savage scowl. 7. Our white-haired prophet of the Great Spirit rebuked him. 8. Kind words are light-winged messengers that soften the hardest hearts. 9. Remember that a heedless, careless word may cause a bitter heart-pang. 10. James Monroe, the fifth President of the United States, died on the fifty-fifth anniversary of American Independence. 11. Many a poor, idle, miserable, pitiable outcast owes his wretchedness to strong drink.

PRONOMINAL ADJECTIVES.

A **Pronominal Adjective** is one which either limits a noun mentioned, or represents a noun understood; as, "*This* task is difficult."—"*This* is a difficult task."

In the first example, *this* "limits" the noun *task*, and is used as an adjective; in the second, *this* "represents" the noun *task*, and is used as a pronoun.

Pronominal adjectives are of three kinds; Distributive, Demonstrative, and Indefinite.

The **Distributive Pronominal Adjectives** are so called because they limit or represent the names of objects taken separately or singly.

The principal *distributives* are *each, every, either,* and *neither*.

The **Demonstrative Pronominal Adjectives** are so called because they limit or represent the names of objects in a definite or particular manner.

The principal *demonstratives* are *this, that, these,* and *those*.

The **Indefinite Pronominal Adjectives** are so called because they limit or represent the names of objects in an indefinite manner.

The principal *indefinites* are *all, another, any, none, one, other, some, such.*

The following may also be classed among the pronominal adjectives: *both, enough, few, former, latter, little, less, least, much, many, more, most, same, several,* and a few others.

Which and *what,* and their compounds, are *pronominal adjectives* when used to limit nouns; as, "The sun gives light by day; *which fact* is obvious."

Which and *what,* and their compounds, are *interrogative pronominal adjectives* when placed before nouns to ask questions; as, "*What* books have you lost?"—"*Which* question do you not understand?"

EXERCISE I.—Write ten sentences, containing different distributives;—ten, containing different demonstratives;—ten, containing different indefinites.

EXERCISE II.—Name the *pronominal adjectives* in the following sentences, tell to which *class* each belongs, and give the reasons:—

MODEL.—"This problem is less difficult than that is."

This.—"This" is a pronominal adjective, because it *limits* the noun *problem ;* it is a *demonstrative pronominal adjective,* because it limits the name of an object in a definite manner.

That.—"That" is a pronominal adjective, because it *represents* the noun *problem ;* it is a *demonstrative pronominal adjective,* because it represents the name of an object in a definite manner.

1. Every man has some good qualities. 2. The same duties were expected of each. 3. They lay down to sleep, each clasping the other in his arms. 4. Every spot to which these little ones would probably have strayed, was searched. 5. Neither statement seemed true, but, as no other was offered in its place, we were obliged to accept it. 6. Few of us do what we are able to do. 7. In such a peaceful village there was no need of those precautions. 8. Enough can not be done to repay his kindness. 9. O, what agony filled the heart of the mother! 10. The two runners started; each, without any effort, kept by the side of the other until near the end of the race, when both put forth their utmost energies to win.

COMPARISON OF ADJECTIVES.

Many adjectives, chiefly the common adjectives, are capable of Comparison.

The **Comparison** of an adjective is the changes of its form to denote different degrees of quality.

Adjectives have three degrees of comparison; the Positive, the Comparative, and the Superlative.

The **Positive Degree** is that form of an adjective which is used to denote simply a quality; as, *wise, happy, small.*

The **Comparative Degree** is that form of an adjective which is used to denote a higher or a lower quality than the positive; as, *wiser, happier, smaller.*

The **Superlative Degree** is that form of an adjective which is used to denote the highest or the lowest quality of all compared; as, *wisest, happiest, smallest.*

THE FORMATION OF COMPARATIVES AND SUPERLATIVES.

Adjectives of one syllable are generally compared by suffixing to the positive *er* to form the comparative, and *est* to form the superlative.

Thus, pos. *sweet*, comp. *sweeter*, sup. *sweetest.*

Adjectives of more than one syllable are generally compared by placing before the positive *more* or *less* to form the comparative, and *most* or *least* to form the superlative.

Thus, pos. *truthful*, comp. *more truthful*, sup. *most truthful*; pos. *pleasant*, comp. *less pleasant*, sup. *least pleasant.*

Dissyllables ending with *y* or *e* are generally compared by suffixing to the positive *er* to form the comparative, and *est* to form the superlative.

Thus, pos. *lovely*, comp. *lovelier*, sup. *loveliest*; pos. *simple*, comp. *simpler*, sup. *simplest.*

IRREGULAR COMPARISON.

The following adjectives are compared irregularly:—

Positive.	Comparative.	Superlative.
Good,	better,	best.
Bad, evil, *or* ill,	worse,	worst.
Much, *or* many,	more,	most.
Little,	less,	least.

The following are compared both regularly and irregularly:—

Positive.	Comparative.	Superlative.
Near,	nearer,	nearest, next.
Late,	later, latter,	latest, last.
Old,	older, elder,	oldest, eldest.

REMARK.—Numeral adjectives, most proper and pronominal adjectives, those denoting *material, position,* or *shape,* and a few others, such as *whole, universal, exact, supreme,* etc., by reason of their use and meaning, are not compared.

EXERCISE I.—*Compare* such of the following *adjectives* as admit comparison:—

Able, ill, sweet, humble, pleasant, juicy, sour, soft, generous, few, handsome, dry, many, certain, old, round, late, acceptable, thoughtless, lovely, warm, timid, diligent, cheerful, brave, tough, ill-mannered, universal, supreme, good-natured, perfect, English, American, sad, evil-minded, preferable.

EXERCISE II.—Use *adjectives* before the following *nouns,* and tell to what class each adjective belongs:—

Sun, moon, nation, army, navy, prairie, rock, tree, lake, river, soldiers, commander, industry, obedience, happiness, war, books, face, pride, home, life, death, tyrant, pleasure, mountain, valley, ocean, mind, tiger, deer, rose, lily, Franklin, Napoleon.

EXERCISE III.—*Parse* the *adjectives* in the following sentences:—

MODELS.—"Two faithful friends were they."

Two.—Two *friends.*—"Two" is a numeral adjective, "A Numeral Adjective is one, etc.";—cardinal, because it denotes how many it can not be compared; it limits the noun *friends*.

Faithful.—Faithful *friends.*—" Faithful" is an adjective, "An Adjective is a word, etc.";—it can be compared (pos. *faithful*, comp. *more faithful*, sup. *most faithful*);—in the positive degree; it describes the noun *friends*.

2.—"This fact is less important than that is."

This.—This *fact.*—"This" is a demonstrative pronominal adjective, "The Demonstrative Pronominal Adjectives are so called, etc."; it can not be compared; it limits the noun *fact*.

That.—That (*fact*) *is.*—"That" is a demonstrative pronominal adjective, "The Demonstrative Pronominal Adjectives, etc.";—in this sentence it represents the noun *fact;* it is therefore in the singular number, third person, and of the neuter gender;—in the nominative case, because it is the subject of the verb *is*.

1. Tall houses make the street gloomy. 2. The true hero appears in the great, wise man of duty. 3. A little flower sprang up amidst the coarse weeds of a long-neglected garden. 4. The plant raised its beautiful head, and its delicate buds burst forth in gladness. 5. Autumn winds strew the ground with a soft carpet of leaves. 6. An avaricious man uses every effort to make money, but he can not enjoy his ill-gotten wealth. 7. These wishes had long been indulged. 8. Crusoe passed many years on that desert island. 9. All honorable means should be used to advance. 10. More than four thousand years have passed since this world was created. 11. Either course is better than remaining in idleness. 12. Shakspeare stands above all other poets, above all other human writers.

EXERCISE IV.—Parse the nouns, the pronouns, and the articles in the preceding sentences.

VERBS.

A **Verb** is a word used to assert action, being, or state; as, "James *runs.*"—"I *am* here."—"He *sleeps.*"

In these sentences, *runs* asserts *action* of the subject *James; am* asserts *being* of the subject *I;* and *sleeps* asserts *state* of the subject *he;*—*runs, am,* and *sleeps* are therefore *verbs*.

Verbs are the most important words in the language, be-

CLASSES OF VERBS ACCORDING TO MEANING.

cause no sentence can be made to express complete sense without the use of a verb.

EXERCISE.—Name the *verbs* and their *subjects* in the following sentences, and give the reasons:—

MODEL.—"James studies diligently."

Studies.—James studies.—"Studies" is a verb, "A Verb is a word, etc.";
it is a verb because it asserts action. Its subject is *James*, because the action expressed by the verb is asserted of James.

1. The birds fly. 2. John is here. 3. The moonbeams rest upon the plain. 4. Flowers bloom by the house. 5. It rains fast. 6. She whispered in low tones. 7. Winter passed, and spring came. 8. How far it flew! 9. The moon now rose. 10. The whole crew perished. 11. Farmers cultivate the ground. 12. Misfortune comes to all. 13. He followed good examples. 14. He lost his hold, and fell. 15. Sword clashed against sword. 16. With the spring his health returned. 17. I remember it well. 18. All consented to the plan. 19. A wood fire blazed upon the hearth.

CLASSES OF VERBS ACCORDING TO MEANING.

Verbs are divided into two classes, according to their use or meaning; Transitive and Intransitive.

A **Transitive Verb** is one which has an object, or which requires an object to complete the sense.

Thus, "He *saw* the *eagle*."—"The earth *hath bubbles*, as the water *has* (*bubbles*)."

An **Intransitive Verb** is one which has no object, or which does not require an object to complete the sense.

Thus, "Birds *fly*."—"Truth *is* mighty."—"He opened his eyes and *saw*."—"Experience *teaches* better than books."

A transitive verb asserts *action* only, and such *action* as is always exerted upon some person or thing called the *object;* as, "The sun *warms* the *earth*."—"The boy *struck* his *friend*."

An intransitive verb asserts *being* or *state*,—or *action* not exerted upon any person or thing; as, "The sky *is* clear."—"The traveler *sits* by the roadside."—"The wind *blows*."

EXERCISE I.—Mention the verbs in the following sentences, tell to which *class*, according to meaning, each belongs, and give the reasons:—

MODEL.—"James studies his lessons, while John is idle."

Studies.—Studies *lessons.*—"Studies" is a verb, "A Verb is a word, etc.";—it is transitive, because it has an object (*lessons*).

Is.—"*Is*" is a verb, "A Verb is a word, etc."; it is intransitive, because it has no object.

1. Labor sweetens pleasure. 2. He is a bold speaker. 3. They answer my questions. 4. A good tree bears good fruit. 5. A storm gathered in the west. 6. The firmament proclaims its great Original. 7. Breezes played among the foliage. 8. A certain man had two sons. 9. Show charity to all men. 10. Charity thinketh no evil. 11. My Uncle Toby went to his bureau. 12. The pulse fluttered, then stopped. 13. The camel carried him safely. 14. Captain Cook sailed around the world.

EXERCISE II.—Write ten sentences, each containing a *transitive* verb;—ten, each containing an *intransitive* verb.

PROPERTIES OF VERBS.

The properties of verbs are Voice, Mode, Tense, Number, and Person.

VOICE.

Voice is that property of a transitive verb which shows whether the subject or nominative *does* or *receives* the action expressed by the verb.

Voice belongs to transitive verbs only.

There are two voices; the Active and the Passive.

The **Active Voice** is that form of a transitive verb which shows that the *subject does* the action expressed by the verb; as, "Henry *carries* the *basket.*"

In this sentence, the subject *Henry* does the action expressed by the verb *carries.* "Carries" is, therefore, in the active voice.

The **Passive Voice** is that form of a transitive verb which shows that the *subject receives* the action expressed by the verb; as, "The *basket is carried* by Henry."

In this sentence, the subject *basket* does not act, but receives the action expressed by the verb *is carried*. "Is carried" is, therefore, in the passive voice.

REMARK.—Although intransitive verbs have no voice, yet they have the *form* of the *active* voice.

EXERCISE I.—Name the verbs in the following sentences, tell which are *transitive* and which *intransitive;* tell in what *voice* each is, and give the reasons:—

MODEL.—"The vessel sank soon after it was struck, and carried the crew to the bottom."

Sank.—"Sank" is a verb, "A Verb is a word, etc."; it is intransitive, because the action which it asserts, is not exerted upon any object; it has no voice, because it is an intransitive verb.

Was struck.—"Was struck" is a verb, "A Verb is a word, etc."; it is transitive, because the action which it asserts, is exerted upon some object;—in the passive voice, because it shows that the *subject* (*it*) *receives* the action asserted.

Carried.—Carried *crew.*—"Carried" is a verb, "A Verb is a word, etc."; it is transitive, because the action which it asserts is exerted upon some object (*crew*);—in the active voice, because it shows that the *subject* (*vessel*) *does* the action asserted.

1. A moan was heard. 2. Heroes fought and bled. 3. Armies are defeated. 4. Thick clouds obscured the sun. 5. Trees overhang the brook. 6. Actions are governed by circumstances. 7. The voyage was undertaken at an evil time. 8. He was educated at Yale College. 9 Old letters become very dear to us. 10. The Arago landed me at New York. 11. I was awaked by a loud knock at the door. 12. The bayonet receives its name from Bayonne in France. It was first used in 1603. 13. The first printing-press in America was established in 1639, at Cambridge.

EXERCISE II.—Write ten or more sentences, each containing a verb in the *active voice*.

Change the sentences just written, so that the verb shall be in the *passive voice*. Thus, Active Voice, "A smile *disarms* revenge"; Passive Voice, Revenge *is disarmed* by a smile."

MODE.

Mode is that property of a verb which distinguishes *in what manner* the action the being, or the state, asserted by the verb, is expressed.

Verbs have five modes; the Indicative, the Potential, the Subjunctive, the Imperative, and the Infinitive.

The **Indicative Mode** is that form of the verb which is used to express a *positive assertion;* as, "Washington *commanded* the Americans."

A verb in the indicative mode may also be used to ask a question, and to express uncertainty or contingency; as, "If he *has gone*, I do not know it." "Who *invented* the art of printing?"

The **Potential Mode** is that form of the verb which is used to express *possibility, liberty, power, necessity,* or *desire;* as, "I *can go*."—"He *must study*."

A verb in the potential mode may also be used to ask a question, and to express uncertainty or contingency; as, "*May* I *go?*"—If I *may go*, I certainly *will* (*go*)."

The **Subjunctive Mode** is that form of the verb which is used to express the action, the being, or the state, asserted by the verb, as *desirable, uncertain,* or as *subject to some condition;* as, "If he *come*, he will be received."—"O that I *were* happy!"

A verb in the subjunctive mode always depends upon a verb in some other mode, and is connected with it by one of the conjunctions *if, although, unless, lest,* and *that.*

The **Imperative Mode** is that form of the verb which is used to express *entreaty, permission, command,* or *exhortation;* as, "*Grant* my request."—"*Obey* me."

The subject of a verb in the imperative mode, which is

either *thou* or *you*, is usually omitted, but it must be mentioned in parsing.

The Infinitive Mode is that form of the verb which is used to express an action, a being, or a state, which is *not limited to a subject;* as, "*To love.*"—"He tries *to study.*"

REMARKS.

A verb is said to be *finite* when the action, the being, or the state, which it asserts, is limited to a subject, or nominative.

Verbs in the indicative mode, in the potential, in the subjunctive, and in the imperative, are finite verbs.

A verb in the infinitive mode is not finite, because it has no subject or nominative.

EXERCISE I.—Name each *verb* in the following sentences, the *class* to which it belongs, its *voice* and *mode*, and give the reasons:—

MODEL.—"Night had dropped its black curtain upon the great city."

Had dropped.—Had dropped *curtain.*—"Had dropped" is a verb; "A Verb is, etc."; it is transitive, because it has an object (*curtain*); —in the active voice, because it shows that the subject (*night*) does the action asserted by the verb;—in the indicative mode, because it is used to express a positive assertion.

1. The wind began to blow. 2. Employ time profitably. 3. If he be respected, he will be contented. 4. Evil may befall us. 5. Waves rise and fall. 6. They were injured by the accident. 7. Will you trust me? 8. Friends should tell each other kindly of faults. 9. A quiet tongue prevents strife. 10. They went to travel in foreign lands. 11. No one has lived too long to learn. 12. We can stop under that tree for shelter. 13. We can not easily free ourselves from bad habits. 14. If a book be lost, it must be replaced.

EXERCISE II.—Write sentences, containing verbs in the various modes.

TENSE.

Tense is that property of the verb which distinguishes the *time* of the action, the being, or the state, asserted by the verb.

There are six tenses; the Present, the Past, the Future, the Present Perfect, the Past Perfect, and the Future Perfect.

The **Present Tense** is that form of the verb which is used to express *present time;* as, "I *learn.*"—"Thou *art loved.*"—"He *is writing* a letter."

The present tense denotes what *now is*, what *now takes place*, or what *is now taking place*.

The **Past Tense** is that form of the verb which is used to express *past time;* as, "He *was* a good man."—"He *fought* a battle."—"He *was* dying."

The past tense denotes what *was*, what *took place*, or what *was taking place*.

The **Future Tense** is that form of the verb which is used to express *future time*, merely; as, "I *shall learn.*"—"Spring *will come.*"

The future tense denotes what *shall* or *will be*, what *shall* or *will take place*, or what *shall* or *will be taking place*.

The **Present Perfect Tense** is that form of the verb which is used to express *past time connected with the present;* as, "I *have learned.*"—"Thou *hast been loved.*"—"He *has written* a letter *to-day.*"

The present perfect tense denotes what *has been*, what *has taken place*, or what *has been taking place*, during a period of time of which the present moment is a part.

The **Past Perfect Tense** is that form of the verb which is used to express *past time which is previous to some other past time;* as, "He *had gone, before* the messenger *arrived.*"

The past perfect tense denotes what *had been*, that *had taken place*, or what *had been taking place*, before some past event mentioned.

The Future Perfect Tense is that form of the verb which is used to express *future time which is previous to some other future time;* as, "I *shall have finished* the task *before* the *close of next week.*"

The future perfect tense denotes what *shall* or *will have been,* what *shall* or *will have taken place,* or what *shall* or *will have been taking place,* before some future event mentioned.

THE TENSES OF THE DIFFERENT MODES.

The indicative mode has all the six tenses.
The potential mode has four tenses; the *present*, the *past*, the *present perfect,* and the *past perfect.*
The subjunctive has two tenses; the *present* and the *past.*
The infinitive mode has two tenses; the *present* and the *present perfect.*
The imperative mode has but one tense; the *present.*

EXERCISE I.—Name the *verbs* in the following sentences, tell the class to which each belongs, its *voice, mode,* and *tense,* and give the reasons:—

MODEL.—"Long icicles glistened in the sunlight."
Glistened.—"Glistened" is a verb, "A Verb is, etc."; it is intransitive, because it has no object; it has no voice, because it is an intransitive verb; it is in the indicative mode, because it is used to express a positive assertion;—in the past tense, because it expresses past time.

1. Thirst causes agony. 2. The two friends talked long together. 3. My request has been granted. 4. Trials will come to us all. 5. When I got, the coach had arrived. 6. Woes cluster; they love a train. 7. Take care of the pence, and the pounds will take care of themselves. 8. They will have finished the house before the occupants enter it. 9. The driver carried them all to the hotel. 10. Dingy houses looked down upon the

filthy street. 11. A loud knock was heard. 12. Calmness in danger has saved many. 13. He who will make no effort to gain friends, can not expect sympa hy. 14. We were guarded in our language. 15. They had been reproved often, before they ceased to annoy.

EXERCISE II.—Write sentences containing verbs in the various tenses.

NUMBER AND PERSON.

Verbs have changes of form to correspond with the number and the person of their subjects.

Verbs, therefore, are said to have two numbers, the Singular and the Plural; and three persons,— the First, the Second, and the Third; thus:—

	Singular.	*Plural.*	*Singular.*	*Plural.*
1st Pers.	I am,	We are,	I learn,	We learn,
2d Pers.	thou art,	you are,	thou learnest,	you learn,
3d Pers.	he is;	they are.	he learns;	they learn.

A verb in the infinitive mode has no number or person, because it has no subject.

Some verbs can be used only in one person; as, "It *rains.*" They are called *Unipersonal Verbs.*

PARTICIPLES.

A **Participle** is a form of the verb which has the nature partly of the verb and partly of the adjective; as, "Wealth *acquired* dishonestly, affords no happiness."

The participle has the nature of the verb, because it *expresses* (though it does not *assert*) action, being, or state, and also *implies time.* It has the nature of the adjective, because, like an adjective, it describes or limits a noun or a pronoun.

There are three participles; the Imperfect, the Perfect, and the Preperfect.

The **Imperfect Participle** is one which represents an action, a being, or a state, as *continuing,* or as *un-*

finished; as, "The waves were heard *breaking* on the beach."

The imperfect participle in the active voice ends with *ing* as, *learning, seeing.* In this voice it is a *single* word.

The imperfect participle in the passive voice has *being* for its sign; as, *being seen, being read.* In this voice it is always *complex* in form.

The **Perfect Participle** is one which represents an action, a being, or a state, as *complete* or *finished;* as, "He came, *accompanied* by his friends."—"The army retired, *defeated* on all sides."

The perfect participle in each voice is a single word.

The perfect participle of regular, and of most irregular, verbs, has the same form as the past tense.

They are thus distinguished: The past tense of a verb always *asserts* action, being, or state, *of some subject;* as, "Washington *loved (verb)* his country."

The perfect participle *implies* or *denotes* action, being, or state, but *does not assert it* of any subject; as, "Washington died, *loved (perf. part.)* by his countrymen."

The **Preperfect Participle** is one which represents an action, a being, or a state, as *complete* or *finished before some other action, being,* or *state;* as, "*Having reached* the summit, they *sat* down to rest."

The preperfect participle is always *complex* in form, and in the active voice is made by placing *having,* and in the passive voice by placing *having been,* before the perfect participle; as, *having loved; having been taught.*

REMARKS.

When a participle is used merely to describe a noun or a pronoun, it is called a *Participial Adjective;* as, "*Cultivated* fields surrounded the mansion."—"A *running* stream is a pleasant sight."

When a participle receives a prefix not found in the verb

from which it is formed, it becomes an adjective simply, and is to be parsed as such; as, *beloved, unloved, unhonored.*

When a participle ending with *ing* is used as the name of an action, a being, or a state, it is called a *Participial Noun*, and is parsed as a noun simply; as, "His *reading* is indistinct."

EXERCISE I.—Name the *participles* in the following sentences, and tell to which *class* each belongs; also, the participles used as *adjectives*, and those used as *nouns:*—

MODEL.—"The sentinel, listening to the dashing waves, was lulled into an untroubled sleep."

Listening.—"Listening" is a participle, "A Participle is a form, etc."; it is the imperfect participle of the verb "to listen," because it represents an *action* as continuing or as unfinished.

Dashing.—"Dashing" is the imperf. part. of the verb "to dash"; it is used as an adjective, because it merely describes the noun *waves.*

Untroubled.—"Untroubled" is an adjective, because it is formed from the verb "to trouble" by receiving the prefix *un-*, and is used to describe the noun *sleep.*

1. The old homestead, once so loved and treasured, was now deserted. 2. The whispering winds came through the raised window. 3. Pure and white lay the untrodden snow. 4. The canoe, borne into the seething rapids, was soon carried over the falls. 5. The lamps having been extinguished, darkness enveloped all in its thickening gloom. 6. Having convicted the prisoners by mock law, the council hurried them to undeserved punishment. 7. He lay like a warrior taking his rest. 8. Being accused unjustly, he felt aggrieved. 9. The unbounded prospect lay before us. 10. The general, having received orders calling for men, sent them, by forced marches, to aid the besieging troops. 11. Emerging from the gorge, they found the enemy drawn up in battle array upon elevated ground. 12. Reading makes a full man; writing, an exact man.

EXERCISE II.—Write sentences, containing the different participles;—others containing participial adjectives;—others containing participial nouns.

CLASSES OF VERBS ACCORDING TO FORMATION.

Verbs are divided, according to their formation, into two classes; Regular and Irregular.

CLASSES OF VERBS ACCORDING TO FORMATION.

A **Regular Verb** is one whose past tense and perfect participle are formed by suffixing *ed* to its present tense; as, Pres., *love;* Past, *loved;* Perf. Part., *loved.*

An **Irregular Verb** is one whose past tense or perfect participle, or both, are not formed by suffixing *ed* to its present tense; as, Pres., *take;* Past, *took;* Perf. Part., *taken.*

THE PRINCIPAL PARTS OF VERBS.

The *present tense*, the *past tense*, and the *perfect participle*, are called the Principal Parts of a verb.

They are called the **Principal Parts**, because, besides being themselves tenses or parts of the verb, they aid in the formation of all the other tenses or parts of the verb.

A TABLE OF THE PRINCIPAL PARTS OF THE MORE IMPORTANT IRREGULAR VERBS.

Present.	Past.	Perfect Part.
Abide,	abode,	abode.
Am,	was,	been.
Arise,	arose,	arisen.
Awake,	awoke, awaked,	awaked.
Bear (*to bring forth*),	bore, bare,	born.
Bear (*to carry*),	bore,	borne.
Beat,	beat,	beat, beaten.
Begin,	began,	begun.
Bend,	bended, bent,	bended, bent.
Beseech,	besought,	besought.
Bid,	bid, bade,	bid, bidden.
Bind,	bound,	bound.
Bite,	bit,	bitten, bit.
Bleed,	bled,	bled.
Blow,	blew,	blown.
Break,	broke,	broken.
Breed,	bred,	bred.
Bring	brought,	brought.

Present.	Past.	Perfect Part.
Burst,	burst,	burst.
Buy,	bought,	bought.
Cast,	cast,	cast.
Catch,	caught, catched,	caught, catched
Choose,	chose,	chosen, chose.
Cleave (*to split*),	cleft, clove,	cleft, cloven.
Cling,	clung,	clung.
Clothe,	clothed, clad,	clothed, clad.
Come,	came,	come.
Cost,	cost,	cost.
Creep,	crept,	crept.
Cut,	cut,	cut.
Dare (*to venture*),	dared, durst,	dared.
Dig,	dug, digged,	dug, digged.
Do,	did,	done.
Draw	drew,	drawn.
Dream,	dreamed, dreamt,	dreamed, dreamt.
Drink.	drank,	drunk.
Drive,	drove,	driven.
Dwell,	dwelled, dwelt,	dwelled, dwelt.
Eat,	eat, ate,	eat, eaten.
Fall,	fell,	fallen.
Feed,	fed,	fed.
Feel,	felt,	felt.
Fight,	fought,	fought.
Find,	found,	found.
Flee,	fled,	fled.
Fling,	flung,	flung.
Fly,	flew,	flown.
Forsake.	forsook,	forsaken.
Freeze,	froze,	frozen.
Get,	got,	got, gotten.
Give,	gave,	given.
Go,	went,	gone.
Grow,	grew,	grown.
Hang,	hanged, hung,	hanged, hung.

THE PRINCIPAL PARTS OF IRREGULAR VERBS.

Present.	Past.	Perfect Part.
Have,	had,	had.
Hear,	heard,	heard.
Hide,	hid,	hid, hidden.
Hit,	hit,	hit.
Hold,	held,	held.
Hurt,	hurt,	hurt.
Keep,	kept,	kept.
Know,	knew,	known.
Lay,	laid,	laid.
Lead,	led,	led.
Leave,	left,	left.
Lend,	lent,	lent.
Let,	let,	let.
Lie (*to recline*),	lay,	lain.
Lose,	lost,	lost.
Make,	made,	made.
Mean,	meant,	meant.
Meet,	met,	met.
Mow,	mowed,	mowed, mown.
Pay,	paid,	paid.
Put,	put,	put.
Read,	read,	read.
Ride,	rode,	ridden.
Ring,	rang, rung,	rung.
Rise,	rose,	risen.
Run,	ran, run,	run.
Say,	said,	said.
See,	saw,	seen.
Seek,	sought,	sought.
Sell,	sold,	sold.
Send,	sent,	sent.
Set,	set,	set.
Shake,	shook,	shaken.
Shed,	shed,	shed.
Shine,	shone, shined,	shone, shined.
Shoe,	shod,	shod.

Present.	Past.	Perfect Part.
Shoot,	shot,	shot.
Show,	showed,	shown, showed.
Shrink,	shrunk,	shrunk.
Shut,	shut,	shut.
Sing,	sung, sang,	sung.
Sink,	sunk, sank,	sunk.
Sit,	sat,	sat.
Slay,	slew,	slain.
Sleep,	slept,	slept.
Slide,	slid,	slid, slidden.
Sling,	slung,	slung.
Smite,	smote,	smitten, smit.
Sow,	sowed,	sowed, sown.
Speak,	spoke, spake,	spoken.
Spell,	spelled, spelt,	spelled, spelt.
Spend,	spent,	spent.
Spin,	spun,	spun.
Spread,	spread,	spread.
Spring,	sprung, sprang,	sprung.
Stand,	stood,	stood.
Steal,	stole,	stolen.
Stick,	stuck,	stuck.
Sting,	stung,	stung.
Strike,	struck,	struck, stricken.
String,	strung,	strung.
Strive,	strove,	striven.
Swear,	swore,	sworn.
Sweep,	swept,	swept.
Swell,	swelled,	swelled, swollen.
Swim,	swam, swum,	swum.
Swing,	swung,	swung.
Take,	took,	taken.
Teach,	taught,	taught.
Tear,	tore,	torn.
Tell,	told,	told.
Think,	thought,	thought.

Present.	Past.	Perfect Part.
Thrive,	thrived,	thrived, thriven.
Throw,	threw,	thrown.
Thrust,	thrust,	thrùst.
Tread,	trod,	trod, trodden.
Wear,	wore,	worn.
Weave,	wove,	woven, wove.
Weep,	wept,	wept.
Win,	won,	won.
Work,	worked, wrought,	worked, wrought.
Wring,	wrung,	wrung.
Write,	wrote,	written.

AUXILIARY VERBS.

An Auxiliary Verb is one which helps to form the modes and the tenses of other verbs.

The auxiliary verbs are *be, do, have, will, can, may, shall, must,* and *need.*

THE USES OF AUXILIARY VERBS.

Be, do, have, need, and *will,* are also complete or principal verbs; they are auxiliary, when used with a participle or with any other part of a principal verb.

Can, may, must, and *shall,* are auxiliary verbs only.

Be, and its variations (*am, art, is, are, was, wast, were, wert, been, being*), when used with the perfect participle of a principal verb, form the passive voice of that verb; as, "I am *loved.*"—"If I *be loved.*"

When used with the imperfect participle of a principal verb, they form what is called the *Progressive Form* of that verb; as, "Thou *art studying.*"

Do, in the active voice, makes what is called the *Emphatic Form* of the present tense in the indicative mode, in the subjunctive, and in the imperative; as, "They *do wish* to go."

In the passive voice, the emphatic form is used in the imperative mode only; as, "*Do* thou *be loved.*"

F

Did, the past form of *do*, in the active voice makes the emphatic form of the past tense in the indicative mode and in the subjunctive; as, "I know that he *did intend* to go."

Did is not used in the passive voice.

Have helps to form the present perfect tense; and its past, *had*, the past perfect; as, "I *have lived.*"—"We *had seen.*"

Will and *shall* help to form the future tense; and *will have* and *shall have*, to form the future perfect tense; as, I *shall* or *will write.*"—"He *shall have written.*"

Can, may, must, and *need,* help to form the present tense of the potential mode; as, "I *can, may, must,* or *need write.*"

Can have, may have, must have, and *need have,* help to form the present perfect tense of the potential mode; as, "Thou *mayst have been* there."

Might, could, would, and *should* (the past of *may, can, will,* and *shall,*) help to form the past tense of the potential; as, "He *might remain.*"

Might have, could have, would have, and *should have,* help to form the past perfect of the potential; as, "I *could have told.*"

CONJUGATION.

The Conjugation of a verb is the regular arrangement of its several *voices, modes, tenses, numbers,* and *persons.*

CONJUGATION OF THE INTRANSITIVE VERB TO BE.

PRINCIPAL PARTS.

Present.—Am.   *Past.*—Was.   *Perfect Participle.*—Been.

INDICATIVE MODE.

Present Tense.

Singular.	Plural.
1. I am,	1. We are,
2. Thou art,	2. You are,
3. He is;	3. They are.

Past Tense.

Singular.	Plural.
1. I was,	1. We were,
2. Thou wast,	2. You were,
3. He was;	3. They were.

Future Tense;—implying simply *future time.*

1. I shall be,	1. We shall be,
2. Thou wilt be,	2. You will be,
3. He will be;	3. They will be.

Future Tense;—implying *promise, command,* or *threat.*

1. I will be,	1. We will be,
2. Thou shalt be,	2. You shall be,
3. He shall be;	3. They shall be.

Present Perfect Tense.

1. I have been,	1. We have been,
2. Thou hast been,	2. You have been,
3. He has been;	3. They have been.

Past Perfect Tense.

1. I had been,	1. We had been,
2. Thou hadst been,	2. You had been,
3. He had been;	3. They had been.

Future Perfect Tense.

1. I shall *or* will have been,	1. We shall *or* will have been,
2. Thou wilt *or* shalt have been,	2. You will *or* shall have been,
3. He will *or* shall have been;	3. They will *or* shall have been.

POTENTIAL MODE.
Present Tense.

1. I may be,	1. We may be,
2. Thou mayst be,	2. You may be,
3. He may be;	3. They may be.

Past Tense.

1. I might be,	1. We might be,
2. Thou mightst be,	2. You might be,
3. He might be;	3. They might be.

Present Perfect Tense.

Singular.
1. I may have been,
2. Thou mayst have been,
3. He may have been;

Plural.
1. We may have been,
2. You may have been,
3. They may have been.

Past Perfect Tense.

1. I might have been,
2. Thou mightst have been,
3. He might have been;

1. We might have been,
2. You might have been,
3. They might have been.

EXERCISE.—Conjugate the verb "*to be*" in every tense of this mode, using all the auxiliaries.

SUBJUNCTIVE MODE.
Present Tense.

Singular.
1. If I be,
2. If thou be,
3. If he be;

Plural.
1. If we be,
2. If you be,
3. If they be.

Past Tense.

1. If I were,
2. If thou were,
3. If he were;

1. If we were,
2. If you were,
3. If they were.

IMPERATIVE MODE.
Present Tense.

2. { Be, *or* be thou,
     Do be, *or* do thou be;

2. { Be, *or* be you,
     Do be, *or* do you be.

INFINITIVE MODE.

Present Tense.—To be. *Present Perfect Tense.*—To have been.

PARTICIPLES.

Imperfect.—Being. *Perfect.*—Been. *Preperfect.*—Having been.

EXERCISE I.—Mention the *mode*, the *tense*, the *number*, and the *person* of each part of the verb "to be" in the following expressions:—

If he were. Be. To have been. They might have been. You shall have been. We had been. Do you be. If I were. If he be. She may

have been. The men have been. He will be. We were. Thou art.
To be. If thou be. We might be. I may be. They will or shall have
been. Thou hast been.

EXERCISE II.—Name the first persons singular, and the first persons plural, of the indicative mode;—of the potential mode;—of the subjunctive mode.

The second persons singular, and the second persons plural, of the imperative mode;—of the potential;—of the indicative;—of the subjunctive.

The third persons singular, and the third persons plural, of the indicative;—of the imperative;—of the subjunctive;—of the potential.

CONJUGATION OF THE VERB
TO LOVE.

ACTIVE VOICE.

PRINCIPAL PARTS.

Present.—Love.   *Past.*—Loved.   *Perf. Participle.*—Loved.

INDICATIVE MODE.

Present Tense.

Singular.	Plural.
1. I love,	1. We love,
2. Thou lovest,	2. You love,
3. He loves;	3. They love.

Present Tense:—Emphatic Form.

1. I do love,	1. We do love,
2. Thou dost love,	2. You do love,
3. He does love;	3. They do love.

Past Tense.

1. I loved,	1. We loved,
2. Thou lovedst,	2. You loved,
3. He loved;	3. They loved.

Past Tense:—Emphatic Form.

1. I did love,	1. We did love,
2. Thou didst love,	2. You did love,
3. He did love;	3. They did love.

Future Tense:—implying simply *future time.*

Singular.
1. I shall love,
2. Thou wilt love,
3. He will love;

Plural.
1. We shall love,
2. You will love,
3. They will love.

Future Tense:—implying *promise, command,* or *threat.*

1. I will love,
2. Thou shalt love,
3. He shall love;

1. We will love,
2. You shall love,
3. They shall love.

Present Perfect Tense.

1. I have loved,
2. Thou hast loved,
3. He has loved;

1. We have loved,
2. You have loved,
3. They have loved.

Past Perfect Tense.

1. I had loved,
2. Thou hadst loved,
3. He had loved;

1. We had loved,
2. You had loved,
3. They had loved.

Future Perfect Tense.

1. I shall *or* will have loved,
2. Thou wilt *or* shalt have loved,
3. He will *or* shall have loved;

1. We shall *or* will have loved,
2. You will *or* shall have loved,
3. They will *or* shall have loved

POTENTIAL MODE.

Present Tense.

1. I may love,
2. Thou mayst love,
3. He may love;

1. We may love,
2. You may love,
3. They may love.

Past Tense.

1. I might love,
2. Thou mightst love,
3. He might love;

1. We might love,
2. You might love,
3. They might love.

Present Perfect Tense.

1. I may have loved,
2. Thou mayst have loved,
3. He may have loved;

1. We may have loved,
2. You may have loved,
3. They may have loved.

Past Perfect Tense.

Singular.
1. I might have loved,
2. Thou mightst have loved,
3. He might have loved;

Plural.
1. We might have loved,
2. You might have loved,
3. They might have loved

SUBJUNCTIVE MODE.
Present Tense.

1. If I love,
2. If thou love,
3. If he love;

1. If we love,
2. If you love,
3. If they love.

Present Tense:—Emphatic Form.

1. If I do love,
2. If thou do love,
3. If he do love;

1. If we do love,
2. If you do love,
3. If they do love.

Past Tense.

1. If I loved,
2. If thou loved,
3. If he loved;

1. If we loved,
2. If you loved,
3. If they loved.

Past Tense:—Emphatic Form.

1. If I did love,
2. If thou did love,
3. If he did love;

1. If we did love,
2. If you did love.
3. If they did love.

IMPERATIVE MODE.
Present Tense.

2. Love, love thou, *or* do thou love;

2. Love, love you, *or* do you love.

INFINITIVE MODE.

Present Tense.—To love. *Present Perfect.*—To have loved.

PARTICIPLES.

Imperfect.—Loving. *Perfect.*—Loved. *Preperfect.*—Having loved.

EXERCISE I.—Conjugate the verbs *to rule, to listen, to obey, to leave,* and *to sell,* in the active voice, in the same manner as the verb *to love* is conjugated.

EXERCISE II.—Mention the *mode,* the *tense,* the *number,* and the *person,* of each verb in the following expressions:—

They had awaked. Beseech. If they did bind. If thou bled. You might have cast. We may dig. He shall or will have drunk. Thou wilt drive. I had eaten. To have fed. Do thou forsake. If he freeze. They may have gained. You must give. We could have. They might, could, would, or should have kept. He will or shall have known. Thou hadst lain. They shrunk. You teach. Thou mayst have sat. He should sit.

PASSIVE VOICE.

The Passive Voice of a verb is formed by combining with its perfect participle the variations of the auxiliary verb *to be.*

INDICATIVE MODE.
Present Tense.

Singular.
1. I am loved,
2. Thou art loved,
3. He is loved;

Plural.
1. We are loved,
2. You are loved,
3. They are loved.

Past Tense.

1. I was loved,
2. Thou wast loved,
3. He was loved;

1. We were loved,
2. You were loved,
3. They were loved.

Future Tense:—implying simply *future time.*

1. I shall be loved,
2. Thou wilt be loved,
3. He will be loved;

1. We shall be loved,
2. You will be loved,
3. They will be loved.

Future Tense:—implying *promise, command,* or *threat.*

1. I will be loved,
2. Thou shalt be loved,
3. He shall be loved;

1. We will be loved,
2. You shall be loved,
3. They shall be loved.

CONJUGATION OF THE VERB "TO LOVE."

Present Perfect Tense.

Singular.
1. I have been loved,
2. Thou hast been loved,
3. He has been loved;

Plural.
1. We have been loved,
2. You have been loved,
3. They have been loved.

Past Perfect Tense.

1. I had been loved,
2. Thou hadst been loved,
3. He had been loved;

1. We had been loved,
2. You had been loved,
3. They had been loved.

Future Perfect Tense.

1. I shall *or* will have been loved,
2. Thou wilt *or* shalt have been loved,
3. He will *or* shall have been loved;

1. We shall *or* will have been loved,
2. You will *or* shall have been loved,
3. They will *or* shall have been loved.

POTENTIAL MODE.
Present Tense.

1. I may be loved,
2. Thou mayst be loved,
3. He may be loved;

1. We may be loved,
2. You may be loved,
3. They may be loved.

Past Tense.

1. I might be loved,
2. Thou mightst be loved,
3. He might be loved;

1. We might be loved,
2. You might be loved,
3. They might be loved.

Present Perfect.

1. I may have been loved,
2. Thou mayst have been loved,
3. He may have been loved;

1. We may have been loved,
2. You may have been loved,
3. They may have been loved.

Past Perfect.

1. I might have been loved,
2. Thou mightst have been loved,
3. He might have been loved;

1. We might have been loved,
2. You might have been loved,
3. They might have been loved.

SUBJUNCTIVE MODE.
Present Tense.

Singular.	Plural.
1. If I be loved,	1. If we be loved,
2. If thou be loved,	2. If you be loved,
3. If he be loved;	3. If they be loved.

Past Tense.

1. If I were loved,	1. If we were loved,
2. If thou were loved,	2. If you were loved,
3. If he were loved;	3. If they were loved.

IMPERATIVE MODE.
Present Tense.

2. Be loved, be thou loved, *or* do thou be loved. | 2. Be loved, be you loved, *or* do you be loved.

INFINITIVE MODE.

Present Tense.—To be loved. *Present Perfect.*—To have been loved.

PARTICIPLES.

Imperfect.—Being loved. *Perfect.*—Loved. *Preperfect.*—Having been loved.

EXERCISE I.—Conjugate the verbs *to take, to catch, to draw,* and *to hold,* in the passive voice, in the same manner as the verb *to love* is conjugated.

EXERCISE II.—Mention the *voice,* the *mode,* the *tense,* the *number,* and the *person,* of each verb in the following expressions:—

Thou art admired. Do thou be thrown. They are pleased. If they were torn. They might have been struck. You may be injured. We shall have been sunk. He shall be shot. It might be woven. I have been sent. Be thou put. They may have been paid. You could be lost. We were lent. He is hit. If thou were hanged. If he be found. To be clad. I may have been harmed. They might have been chosen.

EXERCISE III.—Parse the *verbs* and the *participles* in the following sentences: —

VERBS—EXERCISES. 93

MODELS.—1. "A large tree, which stood in the field, had been struck by lightning."

Stood.—Which stood.—"Stood" is a verb, "A Verb is a word, etc."; it is intransitive, because it has no object;—irregular, because its past tense and perfect participle are not formed by suffixing *ed* to its present tense (pres. *stand,* past *stood,* perf. part. *stood*);—it has no voice, because it is an intransitive verb;—in the indicative mode, because it expresses a positive assertion;—in the past tense, because it denotes past time;—in the singular number, third person, because its subject *which* is, with which it agrees.

Had been struck.—Tree had been struck.—"Had been struck" is a verb, "A Verb is a word, etc.";—transitive, because, etc.;—irregular, because, etc. (pres. *strike,* past *struck,* perf. part. *struck* or *stricken*);—in the pass. voice, because, etc.;—in the indicative mode, because, etc.;—in the past perfect tense, because, etc.;—in the singular number, third person, because its subject *tree* is, with which it agrees.

2.—"Sleeping, the tired child soon forgot its troubles."

Sleeping.—Child sleeping.—"Sleeping" is a participle, "A Participle is a form, etc."; it is the imperfect participle of the verb *to sleep,* because it represents a state as continuing (imperf. part. *sleeping,* perf. *slept,* preperf. *having slept*); it describes the noun *child.*

*Tired.—*Tired *child.—*"Tired" is the perf. part. of the verb *to tire,* and *used as an adjective;* it can be compared (pos. *tired,* comp. *more tired,* sup. *most tired*); it is in the pos. degree, and describes the noun *child.*

3.—"The dropping of water wears even stones."

*Dropping.—*Dropping *wears.—*"Dropping" is the imperf. part. of the verb *to drop*; it is *used as a noun* in the sing. numb., third pers., and of the neuter gender;—in the nom. case, being the subject of the verb *wears.*

1. Nature abounds in variety. 2. The sun ripens the grains. 3. Every fruit contains an acid. 4. Large streams from little fountains flow. 5. If you know the reason, mention it. 6. The unusual appearance caused much alarm. 7. A little stone can make a great bruise. 8. The sailor-boy dreamed of his distant home. 9. He sat long in the gathering twilight, thinking of his misfortunes. 10. The laws by which God governs the world are unchangeable. 11. When we shall have passed through difficulties, we will be prepared for the pleasures which follow. 12. Be honest, and you will be above suspicion. 13. If thou be firm in the right, then shalt thou be indeed firm. 14. Arnold possessed

talents by which he might have been placed among the first men of his age.

15. Often did I strive for the mastery over my feelings, but as often did I fail. 16. He who fears God does not fear man. 17. You might have seen with what cruelty vengeance inflicts torments. 18. The swallow twittered from the straw-built shed. 19. Now, amazed, he gazed upon the surrounding beauties of the landscape. 20. We should consider time as a trust committed to us by God. 21. Delay not until to-morrow the duties which you can perform to-day. 22. He who proposes his own happiness, but does not put his plans in practice, should reflect that, while he forms his purpose, the day rolls on, and "the night cometh when no man can work."

EXERCISE IV.—Parse the nouns, the pronouns, the articles, and the adjectives, in the preceding sentences.

ADVERBS.

An **Adverb** is a word used to qualify the meaning of a verb, an adjective, or another adverb; as, "The stream flows *rapidly*."—"The air is *very* hot."

In the first sentence, *rapidly* is used with the verb *flows* to describe or qualify the manner in which the action expressed by the verb takes place; therefore, *rapidly* is an *adverb*.

In the second sentence, *very* shows in what degree the quality denoted by the adjective *hot* is considered, and limits or qualifies its meaning; therefore, *very* is an *adverb*.

CLASSES OF ADVERBS.

Adverbs may be divided into five general classes; Adverbs of Manner, of Time, of Place, of Degree, and of Interrogation.

I. Adverbs of **Manner** generally answer to the question *How?* Most of them are formed from adjectives or participles by suffixing *ly;* and a few, by suffixing *how* or *wise.*

Some of the adverbs of manner are *ill, so, thus, well, badly, easily, somehow, likewise, certainly, truly, yes, no*.

II. Adverbs of **Time** generally answer to the question *When? How long? How often?* or *How soon?*

The principal adverbs of time are *already, always, daily, ever, forthwith, lately, now, never, often, seldom, since, then, until, yesterday, yet*, etc.; also, *once, twice,* and *thrice*.

III. Adverbs of **Place** generally answer to the question *Where? Whereabouts? Whence?* or *Whither?*

The principal adverbs of place are *anywhere, downward, hence, here, hither, nowhere, off, out, somewhere, thence, there, upward, where, wherever, yonder,* etc.; also, *first, secondly,* etc.; *singly, doubly,* etc.

IV. Adverbs of **Degree** generally answer to the question *How much?* or *How little?* An adverb of degree usually qualifies an adjective or another adverb.

The principal adverbs of degree are *almost, altogether, as, enough, equally, even, much, more, most, little, less, least, only, quite, scarcely, so, very, wholly,* etc.

V. Adverbs of **Interrogation** are used in asking questions.

The principal adverbs of interrogation are *how, when, whence, where, wherefore, whither, why,* etc.

Adverbs used to connect the parts of a sentence are called *Conjunctive Adverbs*.

The principal are *after, as, before, how, then, till, until, when, where, why,* etc.

COMPARISON OF ADVERBS.

A few adverbs are compared like adjectives by suffixing to the positive *er* to form the comparative, and *est* to form the superlative; as, pos. *soon*, comp. *sooner*, sup. *soonest*.

Most adverbs that end with the syllable *ly* admit the form of comparison made by placing before the positive *more* or *less* to form the comparative, and *most* or *least* to form the superlative.

Thus, pos. *easily*, comp. *more easily*, sup. *most easily;* pos. *frequently*, comp. *less frequently*, sup. *least frequently*.

The following adverbs are compared irregularly:—

Positive.	Comparative.	Superlative.
Badly,	worse,	worst.
Far,	farther,	farthest.
Ill,	worse,	worst.
Little,	less,	least.
Much,	more,	most.
Well,	better,	best.

EXERCISE I.—Tell to which class each of the following *adverbs* belongs, give the reason, and compare such as can be compared:—

MODEL.—*Thus.*—"Thus" is an adverb of manner, because it answers to the question *How?* It can not be compared.

Much.—"Much" is an adverb of degree, because it answers to the question *How much?* or *How little?* It can be compared,—pos. *much*, comp. *more*, sup. *most*.

Why, wholly, singly, always, well, very, yes, yonder, twice, likewise, only, nowhere, often, certainly, never, here, somehow, even, quite, off, truly, homeward, hither, less, enough, lately, wherever, easily, most, then, when, yet.

EXERCISE II.—Write ten sentences, containing adverbs of manner;—ten, of time;—five, of place;—five, of degree;—five, of interrogation.

EXERCISE III.—Parse the *adverbs* in the following sentences:—

MODEL.—"Lament no more the past, but improve the present."

No.—No *more.*—"No" is an adverb, "An Adverb is a word, etc.";—of manner, because it answers to the question *How?*—it can not be compared; it qualifies the adverb *more*.

More.—Lament more.—"More" is an adverb, "An Adverb is a word, etc.";—of degree, because it answers to the question *How much?* or *How little?*—it can be compared (pos. *much*, comp. *more*, sup. *most*); it is in the comparative degree, and qualifies the verb *lament*.

1. He arose at a very early hour. 2. The air is very clear, very still, and tenderly sad in its serene brightness. 3. How seldom a good man inherits honor and wealth! 4. The noblest monuments gradually decay. 5. It is too late for repentance now. 6. They moved so gently that their

footsteps were not heard. 7. In the morning they spoke more calmly. 8. Honesty is often recommended by those who are not honest themselves. 9. They had scarcely reached the ravine when they were furiously attacked. 10. Temptations are not always easily overcome. 11. Long and anxiously did he await their return. 12. A train was rushing along at almost lightning speed. 13. We should grasp at the shadow less eagerly, and we would prize the substance more.

EXERCISE IV.—Parse the nouns, the pronouns, the articles, the adjectives, and the verbs, in the preceding sentences.

PREPOSITIONS.

A **Preposition** is a word used before a noun or a pronoun to show its relation to some preceding word; as, "The ship *in* the harbor will soon sail."

In this sentence, the word *in* is used to show the relation of *harbor* to *ship* with regard to place; therefore *in* is a *preposition*.

CLASSES OF PREPOSITIONS.

Prepositions are divided into three classes: Simple, Compound, and Complex.

The **Simple Prepositions** are nineteen, namely:—*at, after, by, down, for, from, in, of, on, over, past, round, since, through, till, to, under, up, with*.

Compound Prepositions are usually formed by prefixing *a* or *be* to some noun, adjective, adverb, or preposition; by uniting two prepositions; or by uniting a preposition and an adverb.

The compound prepositions formed by prefixing *a* are *abaft, aboard, about, above, across, against, along, amid, amidst, among, amongst, around, athwart*.

The compound prepositions formed by prefixing *be* are *before, behind, below, beneath, beside, besides, between, betwixt, beyond*.

The compound prepositions formed by uniting two prepositions, or a preposition and an adverb, are *into, throughout, toward, towards, underneath, until, unto, upon, within, without.*

Complex Prepositions are composed of two or more prepositions, or of a preposition and some other part of speech, which together express one relation.

Thus, "The spring flowed *from between* the rocks." Here, *from between* is a complex preposition, and shows the relation between *rocks* and *flowed.*

From before, from between, from over, over against, out of, round about, are complex prepositions.

EXERCISE I.—Write ten sentences containing simple prepositions; —ten, compound;—six, complex.

EXERCISE II.—Parse the *prepositions* in the following sentences:—

MODEL.—"They passed from the house, and wandered about the city."

From.—Passed from *house.*—"From" is a simple preposition, "A Preposition is a word, etc."; it is used before the noun *house* to show its relation to the verb *passed.*

About.— Wandered about *city.*—"About" is a preposition, "A Preposition is a word, etc.";—a compound preposition, "Compound Prepositions are usually formed, etc."; it is used before the noun *city* to show its relation to the verb *wandered.*

1. Loud shouts of merriment burst from the happy group. 2. The songs of the birds struck upon his ear as they had in his boyhood. 3. Pride goeth before destruction. 4. The wolves prowled around the house. 5. Nothing great can be accomplished without labor. 6. The orders of the officers were heard above the din of battle. 7. Guard against the sudden impulse of anger.

In the country, close by the road, stood a handsome house. Before it there was a garden with flowers, and a painted railing; and just outside of the railing, among beautiful green grass, grew a little daisy. The sun shone upon it as warmly and kindly as upon the large flowers in the garden.

EXERCISE III.—Parse the nouns, the pronouns, the articles, the adjectives, the verbs, and the adverbs, in the preceding sentences.

CONJUNCTIONS.

A **Conjunction** is a word used to connect the words, the parts of a sentence, or the sentences, between which it is placed; as, "He is patient *and* happy, *because* he is a Christian."

In this example, *and* connects the words *patient* and *happy*, while *because* connects the parts of the sentence, *He is patient and happy*, and *he is a Christian;* the words *and* and *because* are therefore *conjunctions.*

CLASSES OF CONJUNCTIONS.

Conjunctions may be divided into two general classes; Copulative and Disjunctive.

A **Copulative Conjunction** is one which denotes an *addition,* a *consequence,* a *purpose,* a *reason,* or a *supposition.*

The copulative conjunctions are *also, and, as, because, both, even, for, if, seeing, since, so, that, then,* and *therefore.*

A **Disjunctive Conjunction** is one which denotes a *choice,* a *comparison,* a *separation,* or a *restriction.*

The disjunctive conjunctions are *although, but, either, else, except, lest, neither, nevertheless, nor, notwithstanding, or, provided, than, though, unless, yet, whereas,* and *whether.*

EXERCISE I.—Write ten sentences, containing copulative conjunctions;—ten, containing disjunctive conjunctions.

EXERCISE II.—Parse the *conjunctions* in the following sentences:—

MODEL.—"Let your character be pure and upright, that you may deserve the love of your friends."

And.—*Pure* and *upright.*—"And" is a conjunction, "A Conjunction is a word, etc.";—a copulative conjunction, because it denotes *addition;* it connects the words *pure* and *upright* between which it is placed.

That.—*Let your character be pure and upright,* that *you may deserve the ove of your friends.*—"Tha." is a conjunction, "A Conjunction is a word, etc."; —a copulative conjunction, because it denotes a reason; it connects the two sentences *Let your character be pure and upright*, and *you may deserve the love of your friends*, between which it is placed.

1. The farmer sold his wheat and corn to the miller. 2. Rain and sunshine are needed for the growth of crops. 3. Henry came, but he could not remain long. 4. You must treat others kindly if you wish kind treatment. 5. The minutes are precious, therefore improve them. 6. He was faithful and just to me. 7. Judge not, that ye be not judged.

The glorious sun has set, and the air, which was sultry, has become cool. No murmur of bees is around the hive, or among the honeyed woodbines; they have done their work, and lie close in their waxen cells. The smith's hammer is not heard upon the anvil, nor is the harsh saw of the carpenter heard.

EXERCISE III.—Parse all the nouns, the pronouns, the articles, the adjectives, the verbs, the adverbs, and the prepositions, in the preceding sentences.

INTERJECTIONS.

An Interjection is a word used in exclamation, to express some emotion of the mind; as, *Ha! pshaw! alas! halloo!*

The following are interjections:—
Adieu, ah, ahoy, alas, bah, faugh, fie, foh, ha, halloo, hist, ho, humph, pshaw, tush, whist.

EXERCISE I.—Parse the *interjections* in the following sentences:—
MODEL.—"Alas! how vain are our hopes!"
Alas.—"Alas" *has no grammatical connection.*—"Alas" is an interjection, "An Interjection is a word, etc."

1. Adieu! I must go. 2. Hist! avoid all noise. 3. Pshaw! how careless you are! 4. Bah! can he be deceived by such stories? 5. Ah! must we part thus from all that is dear?

EXERCISE II.—Compose sentences, each of which shall contain all the parts of speech.

Parse each word in the sentences composed.

Part Third.

SYNTAX.

SYNTAX treats of sentences, and teaches how to construct them from words.

A **Sentence** is two or more words (one of which must be a finite verb) so combined as to make complete sense; as, "Water flows to seek its level."

The complete sense contained in a sentence is called a **Proposition**.

Thus, "Water flows" is both a *sentence* and a *proposition*.

A **Phrase** is two or more words combined, forming one expression, but not making complete sense.

Thus, "Water flows to seek its level" is a *sentence;*—"*to seek its level*" is a *phrase*, or a part of a sentence.

CLASSES OF SENTENCES ACCORDING TO USE.

Sentences may be divided, according to the manner in which they are used, into Declarative, Interrogative, Imperative, and Exclamatory.

A **Declarative Sentence** is one which is used to affirm or to deny; as, "The sun shines."

An **Interrogative Sentence** is one which is used to ask a question; as, "Does the sun shine?"

An **Imperative Sentence** is one which is used to express a command, an entreaty, or a permission; as, "Let the sun shine."—" Be persuaded."

An **Exclamatory Sentence** is one which is used in

exclamation, or to express strong emotion; as, "How the sun shines!"—"Alas, we are lost!"

EXERCISE I.—Mention to which *class* each of the following sentences belongs, and give the reason:—

MODEL 1.—"The sun gives light."

This is a declarative sentence, because it is one which is used to affirm something.

2.—"Obey your parents."

This is an imperative sentence, because it is one which is used to express a command.

1. The rain falls. 2. The storm has ceased. 3. The dove returned no more. 4. How many pecks are contained in a bushel? 5. Alas! I am ruined. 6. Practise what you preach. 7. How the thunder rolls! 8. Take not the name of God in vain. 9. Remorse will haunt a guilty conscience. 10. Do you know your lesson yet? 11. Bright, in that happy land, beams every eye. 12. In what year did the American Revolution commence? 13. If you wish to be happy, do your duty. 14. How gracefully Mary walks! 15. Let us then be up and doing.

EXERCISE II.—Compose ten *declarative* sentences;—ten *interrogative;*—ten *imperative;*—ten *exclamatory.*

CLASSES OF SENTENCES ACCORDING TO FORM.

Sentences are divided according to their form into Simple, Complex, and Compound.

A **Simple Sentence** is one which contains a single proposition; as, "I will go."

A **Complex Sentence** is one which contains a proposition qualified by one or more other propositions.

Thus, "I will go, *if you stay*," "He *who is diligent*, shall be rewarded," are complex sentences.

One proposition qualifies another, when added to explain it, or to change or complete its meaning.

CLAUSES.—The propositions in complex sentences are called *Clauses.*

Clauses are of two kinds; Independent (or Principal), and Dependent (or Qualifying).

An **Independent Clause** is one which would express complete sense if used alone.

A **Dependent Clause** is one which depends upon another clause and qualifies its meaning.

Thus, in the complex sentence, "I will go, if you stay," *I will go* is the independent clause, and *if you stay* is the dependent.

Clauses are usually connected by *relative pronouns*, by *conjunctive adverbs*, or by the conjunctions *as, for, if, since, so, than, that, though, unless,* and a few others.

A **Compound Sentence** is one which contains two or more sentences, simple or complex.

Thus, "*The trees are shaken by the wind,* and *the leaves strew the ground,*" "*I will go,* but *you must stay until I return,*" are compound sentences.

MEMBERS.—The simple or the complex sentences in a compound sentence are called *Members*.

Thus, in the compound sentence, "I will go, but you must stay until I return," there are two members; the *first* is the simple sentence, *I will go,* and the *second* is the complex sentence, *you must stay until I return.*

Members are usually connected by the conjunctions *also, and, both, but, either, neither, nor, or.*

EXERCISE I.—Classify the following sentences:—
MODEL 1.—"Books afford instruction."
This is a sentence, "A Sentence is two or more words, etc.";—declarative, because it affirms something;—simple, because it contains a single proposition.

2.—"Did you see the gentleman who called yesterday?"
This is a sentence, "A Sentence is two or more words, etc.";—inter-

rogative, because it is used to ask a question;—complex, because i contains a proposition qualified by another proposition.

The independent or principal proposition is, *Did you see the gentleman;* the dependent or qualifying proposition is, *who called yesterday;*—these clauses are connected by the relative *who*.

3.—" The sun sets, and the mountains are shaded."

This is a sentence, "A Sentence is, etc.";—declarative, because, etc.;—compound, because it contains two simple sentences, *The sun sets,* and *the mountains are shaded,*—which are members, connected by the conj. *and.*

1. You must command. 2. I will obey. 3. I will obey if you command. 4. You must command, and I will obey. 5. He recites promptly. 6. He recites well, because he has studied diligently. 7. If you do not succeed at first, try again. 8. There goes the boy that never tells a lie. 9. The cunning man is often caught in his own trap. 10. Oh! what a joyful meeting there will be!

11. Learn one thing at a time, and learn that thing well. 12. This is the difference between Napoleon and Washington: the one fought to be a monarch; the other fought to be a servant. 13. The wicked flee when no man pursueth. 14. When did this accident, which you have related, happen? 15. The mariner's compass was invented before America was discovered. 16. Love not sleep, lest thou come to poverty. 17. After the war had continued nearly eight years, the colonies became independent.

EXERCISE II.—Compose ten *simple* sentences;—ten *complex* sentences;—ten *compound* sentences.

DIVISIONS OF SYNTAX.

Syntax may be considered under two divisions; Analysis and Synthesis.

Analysis, in Grammar, is the separation of sentences into the parts which compose them.

Synthesis is the construction or formation of sentences from words.

ELLIPSIS.—*Ellipsis* is the omission of one or more words, phrases, or clauses necessary to complete the sense and construction of a sentence: as, "He loves play better than (*he loves*) study."

ANALYSIS.

THE PARTS OF SENTENCES.

The Parts of Sentences are the Essential, the Secondary (or Qualifying), the Connecting, and the Independent.

THE ESSENTIAL PARTS.—The Essential Parts are those without which a sentence can not be formed.

The essential parts are the Subject and the Predicate.

The Subject is that of which something is said or asserted; as, "*Water* flows."

The Predicate is that which is said or asserted of the subject; as, "Water *flows*."

A subject and a predicate combined form a proposition or sentence.

EXERCISE I.—Mention the subject and the predicate in each of the following sentences:—

MODEL.—"Water flows."

In this sentence, *water* is the subject, because it is that concerning which *flows* is said or asserted; and *flows* is the predicate, because it is that which is said or asserted of *water*; the two parts combined form the proposition or sentence, "Water flows."

1. Flowers fade. 2. Leaves wither. 3. Winter has come. 4. Children should try. 5. Something has happened. 6. Lessons are recited. 7. Pleasure allures. 8. Study improves. 9. Gold glistens. 10. Charles I. was beheaded. 11. Nations have perished. 12. Sin will be punished.

EXERCISE II.—Mention the subject and the predicate in each of the following sentences:—

MODEL.—"The water of the brook flows into the lake."

In this sentence, *The water of the brook* is the subject, because it is that concerning which *flows into the lake* is asserted; and *flows into the lake* is the predicate, because it is that which is asserted of *the water of the brook;* the two parts combined form the proposition or sentence.

1. The flowers of summer are now blooming. 2. Icy winter will soon be here. 3. She is handsome. 4. A thick fog rests upon the river. 5. Speak (thou) distinctly. 6. Louisiana was purchased from France in 1803. 7. Deceit never prospers. 8. Resist the allurements of sin. 9. Something sad has happened to him. 10. Study improves the mind. 11. The ship was loaded with cotton for Liverpool. 12. To do good is pleasant. 13. Little things are sometimes very important. 14. To be contented is to be happy.

EXERCISE III.—Mention the subject and the predicate in each of the following sentences:—

MODEL.—"Little brooks and tiny streams flow down its side and empty into the lake."

In this sentence, *Little brooks and tiny streams* is the subject, because it is that concerning which *flow down its side and empty into the lake* is asserted; and *flow down its side and empty into the lake* is the predicate, because it is that which is asserted of *little brooks and tiny streams;* the two parts combined form the sentence or proposition.

1. Bricks and mortar form the wall. 2. The sun rises and sets. 3. Leaves and flowers wither and fade. 4. Truth and error can never agree. 5. Charles and William will remain and study. 6. Napoleon fought and conquered. 7. The lion and the lamb shall lie down together. 8. We must labor and wait. 9. Virtue and vice are at variance. 10. Washington and Jefferson were patriots.

DISTINCTIONS OF SUBJECT AND PREDICATE.

The subject may be Simple, Complex, or Compound; as, Simple, *water;* Complex, *the water of the brook;* Compound, *little brooks and tiny streams.*

The predicate may be Simple, Complex, or Compound; as, Simple, *flows;* Complex, *flows down its side;* Compound, *flow and empty.*

THE SIMPLE SUBJECT AND THE SIMPLE PREDICATE.

The **Simple Subject** is usually a noun or a pronoun,

or some word used as a noun; as, "*Water* flows."—"*It* flows."

The simple subject is also called the *subject-nominative.*

The **Simple Predicate** is always and simply a finite verb; as, "Water *flows.*"—"It *might have flowed.*"

The simple predicate is also called the *predicate-verb.*

THE COMPLEX SUBJECT AND THE COMPLEX PREDICATE.

The **Complex Subject** is the simple subject taken with all its qualifications.

The *qualifications* of a word are those words, phrases, or clauses which limit or qualify its meaning or use.

In the sentence, "The water of the brook flows," *water* is the subject-nominative or the simple subject, the article *the* and the phrase *of the brook* are its qualifications;—therefore, *The water of the brook* is the complex subject.

The **Complex Predicate** is the simple predicate taken with all its qualifications.

In the sentence, "The brook flows through the meadow," *flows* is the predicate-verb or simple predicate, and the phrase *through the meadow* is its qualification;—therefore, *flows through the meadow* is the complex predicate.

THE COMPOUND SUBJECT AND THE COMPOUND PREDICATE.

The **Compound Subject** is one which consists of two or more simple or complex subjects, united by one conjunction or more.

In the sentence, "Brooks and streams flow," the subject is compound, consisting of the two simple subjects, *brooks* and *streams,* which are connected by the conjunction *and.*

The **Compound Predicate** is one which consists of two

or more simple or complex predicates, united by one conjunction or more.

In the sentence, "Brooks flow down its side and empty into the lake," the predicate is compound, consisting of two complex predicates united by the conjunction *and*.

THE SECONDARY PARTS.—The *Secondary Parts* of sentences are the words, phrases, and clauses used in forming complex subjects and predicates.

Thus, in the sentence, "*A* love *for pleasure rapidly* increases," *a*, *for pleasure*, and *rapidly* are the *secondary parts*.

THE CONNECTING PARTS.—The *Connecting Parts* of sentences are *relative pronouns, conjunctions*, and *conjunctive adverbs*.

THE INDEPENDENT PARTS.—The *Independent Parts* of sentences are words and phrases which are not essential, secondary, or connecting parts.

1. Words, with or without qualifications, used as the names of persons or things addressed or uttered in exclamation, are independent; as, "*Brother*, give me thy hand."—"*Gentlemen of the jury*, I ask your attention."

2. Interjections and certain adverbs; as, "*Oh!* it is not possible."—"*Well*, I am willing."

EXERCISE.—In the following sentences, (1) mention the *kind* of each; (2) the *subject* and the *predicate* of each; (3) the *kind of subject and predicate;* (4) and the *subject-nominative* and the *predicate-verb*.

MODEL 1.—"Clouds darken."

This is a sentence, declarative, simple. The subject is *clouds*, simple; the predicate is *darken*, simple. The subject-nominative is the noun *clouds;* the predicate-verb is *darken*.

2.—"The heavy clouds darken the air."

This is a sentence, declarative, simple. The subject is *The heavy clouds*, complex; the predicate is *darken the air*, complex. The subject-nominative is the noun *clouds;* the predicate-verb is *darken*.

3.—"Heaven and earth shall pass away."

This is a sentence, declarative, simple. The subject is *Heaven and earth*, compound, consisting of two simple subjects connected by the conjunction *and;* the predicate is *shall pass away*, complex. The subject-nominatives are *heaven* and *earth*, and the predicate-verb is *shall pass*.

4.—"Will James go, if I ask him?"

This is a sentence, interrogative, complex. The independent clause or proposition is, *Will James go?* This is qualified by the dependent clause or proposition, *if I ask him.* They are connected by the conj. *if.*

The subject of the independent clause is *James*, simple; the predicate is *will go*, simple.

The subject of the dependent clause is *I*, simple; the predicate is *ask him*, complex, etc.

5.—"The soil is fertile, but the climate is unhealthy."

This is a sentence, declarative, compound. The members are *The soil is fertile*, and *the climate is unhealthy*. They are connected by the conjunction *but.*

The subject of the first member is *the soil*, complex; the predicate is *is unhealthy*, complex, etc.

1. Dew-drops sparkle. 2. Children play. 3. The hour has passed. 4. Beauty charms us. 5. The fragrant woodbine had clambered over the porch. 6. A deep snow lay upon the ground. 7. A noisy flock of blue-jays collected in the woods behind us. 8. The butter and the cheese of Delaware county are justly celebrated. 9. You must try harder if you wish to succeed. 10. The leaves are falling fast, although the air is still. 11. Do you know where John's folks live? 12. Improve the moments as they pass. 13. The wind was favorable, and the ship soon brought us within sight of land. 14. Righteousness exalteth a nation, but sin is a reproach to any people. 15. The rich man died, and was buried. 16. None of the country-people would venture at night near the old mill, which was said to be haunted. 17. The sun had set behind the western hills, and twilight was gradually deepening into night.

EXERCISE II.—Mention the *independent parts* in the following:—

1. Father, must I stay? 2. Sweet bird, thy bower is ever green. 3. Oh! could I fly, I'd fly with thee. 4. Do you remember, James, what I said? 5. I am here, ladies and gentlemen, to address you. 6. Well, my friend, what can I do for you? 7. O ye little warblers, how sweet are your notes!

THE QUALIFICATIONS OF THE SIMPLE SUBJECT.

The simple subject, if a noun, may be qualified in the following ways:—

1. By an article; as, "*The* hour has come."
2. By an explanatory noun or pronoun in the nominative case; as, "*Friend* William has come."
3. By a noun or a pronoun in the possessive case; as, "*Pleasure's* hour has come."—"*My* hour has come."
4. By a preposition with its object; as, "Hours *of rest*."
5. By an adjective; as, "*Pleasant* hours were spent."
6. By a participle; as, "Hours *appointed* have begun."
7. By a verb in the infinitive mode; as, "Time *to study* has begun."
8. By a clause; as, "Men *who will work*, have come."

When the simple subject is a pronoun, it may have all the qualifications of a noun, except that made by a noun or a pronoun in the possessive case.

Any qualifying word, or two or more words taken as one qualifying term, may be called an *Adjunct*.

Words which qualify the simple subject may themselves be qualified in the ways above mentioned.

The noun or the pronoun used as the name of a person or thing addressed or uttered in exclamation may be qualified like the subject-nominative; as, "O friend *of my boyhood!*"

THE QUALIFICATIONS OF THE SIMPLE PREDICATE.

The simple predicate or predicate-verb may be qualified in the following ways:—

1. By a noun or a pronoun in the nominative case, which means the same person or thing as the subject-nominative; as, "Kings are *men*."—"Napoleon was proclaimed *emperor*."

The predicate-verb is thus qualified only when it is an intransitive verb, or a transitive verb in the passive voice.

This qualifier may be called the *predicate-nominative*.

2. By a noun in the objective case; as, "They found *gold*."

QUALIFICATIONS OF THE SIMPLE PREDICATE. 111

3. By a preposition with its object; as, "He came *to school.*"
4. By an adjective describing or limiting the subject; as, "Truth is *eternal.*"
5. By a participle relating to the subject; as, "He came *running.*"
6. By an adverb; as, "William came *speedily.*"
7. By an infinitive; as, "He came *to see.*"
8. By a clause; as, "I discovered *that I was ignorant.*"

Words which qualify the simple predicate may be qualified just as the same parts of speech in the complex subject are qualified.

An infinitive or a participle may receive all the qualifications that the predicate-verb can take.

EXERCISE I.—Mention (1) the *simple subjects* and *predicates;* (2) their *qualifying words;* (3) the *adjuncts of the qualifying words;* and (4) the *whole* or *complex subjects* and *predicates*, in the following sentences:—

MODEL.—"His very pleasant manners made a favorable impression."

In this sentence the simple subject or subject-nominative is the noun *manners;* the simple predicate or predicate-verb is *made.*

The words qualifying the simple subject or subject-nominative are *his*, a pronoun in the possessive case, and the adjective *pleasant;* and *pleasant* is qualified by the adverb *very.* The whole or complex subject is *His very pleasant manners.*

The word qualifying the simple predicate or predicate-verb is its object, the noun *impression*, which is itself qualified by the article *a* and by the adjective *favorable.* The whole or complex predicate is *made a favorable impression.*

1. Nature is full of variety. 2. Earnest effort rarely fails. 3. William's nobleness of conduct excited much admiration. 4. My name is Norval. 5. Texas was annexed to the United States in 1845. 6. Young persons are fond of novelty. 7. The shores of Lake George are wild and beautiful. 8. Tom pitied her with all his big heart. 9. America has furnished to the world the character of Washington. 10. The teacher should be quick, precise, earnest, and kind. 11. Write your name, by kindness, love, and mercy, on the hearts of those around you. 12. The study of truth is ever joined with the love of virtue. 13. Truthfulness is

the test of character. 14. Daniel, the farmer's son, became greatly distinguished. 15. The high hills looked so tempting to climb. 16. Bridgeport, a cunning little village, was on the other side of the river. 17. Behind the house was a large cornfield. 18. Forests of standing trees have been discovered in some parts of the world, imbedded in stone.

EXERCISE II.—The following sentences have only simple subjects and predicates; make each subject or predicate complex *by adding qualifying words:*—

1. Boys play. 2. Book delights. 3. Grammar teaches. 4. Storm began. 5. Shouts arose. 6. Camels carry. 7. Paris is. 8. Clock ticks. 9. Washington was. 10. Path led. 11. Reception was given. 12. Noise is heard. 13. Squirrel hopped. 14. Deer ran. 15. This happened. 16. Words are spoken. 17. Drink refreshed. 18. Field yielded. 19. Oak rears. 20. Sit. 21. Do you see? 22. Mountain stands.

PHRASES AND CLAUSES.

A phrase may be named according to the part of speech to which its leading word belongs, or from the way in which it qualifies.

The following are the principal phrases:—

1. The Appositional or Explanatory; as, " Hope, *the lightener of toil,* inspired us."

2. The Adjective; as, *"Sick at heart,* we ceased to search."

3. The Adverbial; as, *"Far up the mountain side* stood a little cottage."

4. The Infinitive; as, " Rain descends *to water the earth.*"

5. The Participial; as, *"Darting a look of scorn,* the monarch replied."

6. The Absolute; as, *"A storm arising,* we sought shelter."

The leading noun in this phrase may be qualified like a subject-nominative. This phrase is equivalent to a proposition. It is called *absolute,* because it is *absolved* or *loosened from* its form as a proposition, and is made a phrase.

7. The Independent: as, "*O long expected day,* begin."

REMARK.—Of the preceding phrases, the independent qualifies neither subject nor predicate; the absolute, both subject and predicate, or the whole proposition; the others may qualify either subject or predicate.

Dependent clauses may receive special names from their position in sentences, or from the manner in which they qualify.

1. The Relative or Adjective Clause; as, "He *who runs*, may read."—"The wisdom *which is from above*, is first pure."
This is also called the Explanatory Clause.
2. The Adverbial Clause; as, "It lay *where it fell*."—"Look *before you leap*."
Adverbial Clauses are usually connected with the parts which they qualify by conjunctive adverbs.
3. The Comparative Clause, which is introduced by the conjunction *than*; as, "Truth is stranger *than fiction (is)*."

EXERCISE I.—Classify the following sentences, mention the *phrases* and the *clauses* contained in them, and tell what each qualifies:—

MODEL 1.—"Cyrus, the founder of the Persian empire, took Babylon."

This is a simple sentence; it contains a phrase, namely, *the founder of the Persian empire*, which is appositional or explanatory, and qualifies the subject-nominative, *Cyrus*.

2.—"Cyrus, who founded the Persian empire, took Babylon."

This is a complex sentence; it contains a dependent clause, namely, *who founded the Persian empire*, which is relative or explanatory, and qualifies the subject-nominative, *Cyrus*.

1. Paris, the capital of France, is a beautiful city. 2. Fields, rich with ripening harvests, lay beneath us. 3. I had a desire to visit distant lands. 4. Three millions of people, armed in the holy cause of liberty, are invincible. 5. Once upon a time a wonderful magician lived there. 6. Think before you speak. 7. The rose which was plucked this morning has already withered. 8. Injured by the fall, he lay moaning on the ground. 9. Those best can bear reproof who merit praise. 10. The letter being written, Mary took it to the post-office. 11. Greatly to his delight, William found the long-lost book. 12. Wisdom is more to be desired than gold is.

13. Conscious of his guilt, he could not deny the charge. 14. My

presence of mind returning, I demanded his name. 15. Samuel came after the gate was closed. 16. A pretended patriot, he imprisoned the pope. 17. As we proceeded, new wonders presented themselves. 18. He who builds does not always occupy. 19. Pearl, the English for Margaret, is a pretty name. 20. O, childhood's happy hours! how sweet the remembrance!

EXERCISE II.—Write sentences containing the phrases or the clauses above enumerated.

SYNTHESIS.

Synthesis is that division of Syntax which treats of the construction of sentences from words.

It teaches how to put words together properly, according to principles called *Rules of Syntax*.

RULE I.—THE SUBJECT OF A FINITE VERB.

A noun or a pronoun which is the subject of a finite verb is in the nominative case.

NOTES.

1. The subject of a verb is usually a noun or a pronoun; as, "The *hills* are clothed in green."—"*They* wave with ripening grain."

2. The subject of a verb may also be a verb in the infinitive mode, or any word, used as a noun in the nominative case; as, "*To sleep* is refreshing."—"*Them* should never be used for *those*."

3. Nouns in the first or in the second person are never the subjects of finite verbs. (Rule V., Note 1.)

EXERCISE I.—*Correct* the following sentences:—

MODEL.—"James and me are good friends."

This sentence is incorrect, because *me*, which is a pronoun in the *objective* case, is used as the subject of the verb *are*. *Me* should be *I*, and the sentence should be, "James and I are good friends."

RULE II.—THE NOMINATIVE CASE INDEPENDENT.

1. My brother and me have a little garden. 2. I cannot tell whom will be sent. 3. Him and I were present. 4. Whom do you think was chosen? 5. He did not try so hard as them. 6. Who can explain the principle? Me. 7. Mary is not nearly so old as her. 8. Him and her attend the same school. 9. Thomas reads more plainly than him. 10. Them who come late can not be admitted. 11. He can write better than me, but I can draw as well as him.

EXERCISE II.—*Parse* the *subjects* in the following sentences:—

MODEL 1.—"The Spaniards and the Italians formed an alliance."

Spaniards.—Spaniards *formed.*—"Spaniards" is a proper noun, in the plural number, third person, and of the masculine gender; it is in the nominative case, being one of the subjects of the finite verb *formed*, according to Rule I., "A noun or a pronoun, etc."

2.—"To die for one's country is noble."

To die.—To die *is.*—"To die" is an intransitive, regular verb, in the infinitive mode; it is used as a noun in the singular number, third person, and of the neuter gender;—in the nominative case, being the subject of the verb *is*, according to Rule I., "A noun or a pronoun, etc."

1. Our bones give support to our bodies. 2. The Jews were once very powerful. 3. The walls, the beams, and the rafters of a house should be made strong. 4. To waste time is criminal. 5. Washington, Napoleon, and Frederic the Great were early risers. 6. The beaks of birds differ greatly from each other. 7. To expect much from very young minds is foolish. 8. A pennyworth of mirth is worth a pound of sorrow.

Sweet words, kind remarks, and pleasant smiles have cheered many a weary heart. Pearls and rubies are not more precious than are the little kindnesses that even the smallest child can show; and the happiness conferred by them is greater than words can tell.

RULE II.—THE NOMINATIVE CASE INDEPENDENT.

A noun or a pronoun whose case does not depend upon its connection with any other word, is in the nominative case independent.

NOTES.

A noun or a pronoun may be in the nominative case independent;—

I. When it represents a person or thing addressed; as, "My *son*, attend unto my words."

This is *the nominative independent by address*.

II. When it is used in exclamation; as, "O, the happy *days* of childhood!"

This is *the nominative independent by exclamation*.

III. When it is placed before a participle relating to it, and is not the subject of any verb; as, "This *army* being defeated, all hostilities ceased."

This is *the nominative independent before a participle*.

EXERCISE I.—*Correct* the following sentences:—

MODEL.—"Him being absent, nothing was done."

This sentence is incorrect, because *him*, which is a pronoun in the objective case, should be in the nominative case, because it is used independently before the participle *being*. *Him* should be *he*, and the sentence should be, "He being absent, nothing was done."

1. Them being honest, I have no fear. 2. "And thee too, Brutus!" cried Cæsar. 3. Us having returned, the work progressed. 4. O happy us, if this be so! 5. Thee assisting us, we shall succeed. 6. Me having the key, the door could not be opened. 7. O wretched them! what can be done for them? 8. Whom suffering from sickness, the work all fell upon us. 9. O Thee who rulest the world, hear my prayer!

EXERCISE II.—*Parse* the nouns *used independently* in the following sentences:—

MODEL 1.—"Thou shalt suffer, proud man, for this."

Man.—"Man" has no grammatical connection.—"Man" is a common noun, in the singular number, second person, and of the masculine gender; it is in the nominative case independent by address, according to Rule II., "A noun or a pronoun whose case does not depend, etc."

2.—"France having acknowledged their independence, great rejoicing followed."

France.—"France" has no grammatical connection.—"France" is a proper noun, in the singular number, third person, and of the neuter gender; it is in the nominative case independent before the participle *having acknowledged*, according to Rule II., "A noun or a pronoun, etc."

1. Oh, Hubert, save me from these men! 2. How is your health, my dear friend? 3. Spring returning, the seeds begin to swell in the earth.

4. Ah! my pretty captive, you wished to escape, did you? 5. The bridges being swept away, we could not continue our journey. 6. O deep and dark blue ocean, roll! 7. The summit being gained, they all paused to admire the prospect. 8. Time!—alas! how soon 'tis gone! 9. O Death, come not to me when the beautiful flowers are in bloom. 10. Napoleon having been defeated, the monarchy was re-established. 11. Precious moments! Ah, they will never return. 12. The grave! the grave! It buries every error, and covers every defect.

RULE III.—THE POSSESSIVE CASE.

A noun or a pronoun in the possessive case limits the word used as the name of the thing possessed.

NOTES.

1. The proper forms of nouns and pronouns in the possessive should always be written; as, "The *boy's* hat is lost."—"The *ladies'* dresses were finished."—"This book is *hers.*"

2. The word limited by the possessive may be omitted when its use is not required to complete the sense; as, "The goods were bought at *Stewart's* (store)."

3. In the use of complex nouns, the sign of the possessive is suffixed to the last word of the complex name; as, "Lord *Cornwallis's* troops were surrendered at Yorktown."

4. When two or more nouns in the possessive are connected and denote joint owners of the same thing, the sign of the possessive is suffixed to the last word only.

Thus, "*Ferdinand* and *Isabella's* little fleet";—this implies that both were concerned in the ownership of the fleet.

When two or more nouns in the possessive are connected and denote separate owners of different things, the sign of the possessive is suffixed to each noun.

Thus, "*John's* and *William's* book";—this implies that only one is concerned in the ownership of each book.

EXERCISE I.—*Correct* the following sentences and phrases:—
MODEL 1.—"This book is her's."
This sentence is incorrect, because *her's*, which is in the possessive, has

not the proper form. *Her's* should be *hers*, and the sentence should be "This book is hers."

2.—"David's and Jonathan's friendship."

This phrase is incorrect, because the sign of the possessive is suffixed to each of two nouns connected in the possessive, and denoting joint owners of the same thing. The sign should be suffixed to the last noun only, and the sentence should be, "David and Jonathan's friendship."

1. The boys hat was lost. 2. Mens clothing neatly repaired. 3. Thomas's Jefferson's term as President commenced in 1801. 4. Gates and Burgoyne's troops fought at Saratoga. 5. The books were not their's. 6. Websters Dictionary is a standard work. 7. Who's knives are these? They are our's. 8. Queen's Victoria's reign commenced in 1837. 9. I respect my father as well as my mother's wishes. 10. Mann's and Chase's Arithmetic.

EXERCISE II.—*Parse* the nouns in the *possessive* case in the following sentences:—

MODEL 1.—"He bought the goods at Stewart's."

Stewart's.—Stewart's (*store*).—"Stewart's" is a proper noun, in the singular number, third person, and of the masculine gender; it is in the possessive case, and limits the noun *store* (understood), according to Rule III., "A noun or a pronoun, etc."

2.—"Captain Mayne Reid's stories for boys are very interesting."

Capt. Mayne Reid's.—Capt. Mayne Reid's *stories.*—"Capt. Mayne Reid's" is a complex proper noun, in the singular number, third person, and of the masculine gender; it is in the possessive case, and limits the noun *stories*, according to Rule III., "A noun, etc."

1. Tears were in the little fellow's eyes. 2. The painter's first efforts were poor enough. 3. He stopped at the doctor's, and rang the bell. 4. Murray's and Brown's grammars have long been in use. 5. Bunyan's "Pilgrim's Progress" was written while he was in prison. 6. Mary and Susan's mother died while they were young. 7. The company's largest sailing-vessel was wrecked. 8. George Washington's "Farewell Address" was published in 1796. 9. The stocks were sold at Cooke's.

One day Ellen's brother, Casper, brought home a little wagon, which he had bought at the carpenter's. "O," said Ellen, "I wonder if the little canaries could not be taught to draw this wagon around the room."

"I think that they might," was Casper's reply, "if you could make a harness small enough to fit them."

RULE IV.—THE OBJECTIVE CASE.

A noun or a pronoun which is the object of an action or of a relation, is in the objective case.

Action refers to the action asserted by a *verb*, and *relation* to the relation denoted by a *preposition*.

NOTES.

1. A noun or a pronoun can be the object of an action expressed only by a transitive verb in the active voice; as, "Strive *to perform* your *duties*, and your friends *will respect you*."—"The peasant *lived* a *life* of toil."

2. A noun or a pronoun may also be the object of an action expressed by the *participle* of a transitive verb in the active voice; as, "A lake was seen *reflecting* the *rays* of the sun."

3. An intransitive verb, or the participle of an intransitive verb, should not be used to govern the objective case: thus, "I will sit *me* down to rest," should be, "I will sit down to rest."

4. Some nouns seem to be used without any governing word: thus, "He traveled several *miles* before he overtook the party."

Before such a noun, one of the prepositions *by, during, for, in, of, through,* etc., may be supplied in parsing: thus, "He traveled *through* sixty *miles*, etc."

EXERCISE I.—*Correct* the following sentences:—

MODEL 1.—"His father taught him and I to read."

This sentence is incorrect, because the pronoun *I*, which is in the nominative case, is used as the object of the action expressed by the verb *taught*. *I* should be *me*, and the sentence should be, "His father taught him and me to read."

2.—"The weary pilgrim sat himself down by the wayside."

This sentence is incorrect, because the pronoun *himself* is used as the object of the intransitive verb *sat*; it should be omitted, and the sentence should be, "The weary pilgrim sat down by the wayside."

1. Nothing has been heard of he or his brother. 2. Who have you seen during your visit? 3. Between you and I, he is very much mistaken. 4. Who did they call? I. 5. He that is poor and needy assist. 6. She called somebody, but I do not know who. 7. Not thou only have

warned. 8. There is but little left for you and he to do. 9. Who do you want now? 10. Let that be known only to thee and I. 11. The men were tired, and lay themselves down to sleep.

EXERCISE II.—*Parse* the *objectives* in the following sentences:—

MODEL.—"They commenced their journey, and traveled sixty miles."

Journey.—Commenced journey.—"Journey" is a common noun, in the singular number, third person, and of the neuter gender; it is in the objective case, being the object of the action expressed by the verb *commenced*, according to Rule IV., "A noun or a pronoun, etc.'

Miles.—(*Through*) miles.—"Miles" is a common noun, in the plural number, third person, and of the neuter gender; it is in the objective case, being the object of the relation denoted by the preposition *through* (understood), according to Rule IV., "A noun or a pronoun, etc."

1. I love the pebbly beach and the sunny waves. 2. The children gathered the strawberries which grew in great numbers along the path through the meadow. 3. Daisies reared their heads among the violets. 4. The storm continued several days. 5. They rested an hour under the tree, and then continued their journey. 6. He clapped his hands and laughed aloud for joy. 7. Read good books and avoid bad companions. 8. The regiment marched twenty miles the first day. 9. It is better to rule by love than by fear.

Descending the hill, and crossing the little stream at its base, we presently came to a deserted cabin, probably erected by some earlier settler. Here we determined to pass the night.

RULE V.—APPOSITION.

A noun or a pronoun put in apposition with another is in the same case.

NOTES.

1. A noun or a pronoun is put in *apposition*, when it is used with another noun or pronoun to explain it, or when it is added or repeated for the sake of emphasis.

Thus, "Franklin, the *philosopher*, will ever be remembered."—"Spring, joyous *spring*, has come."—"We, the *people* of the United States."

2. The proper name and the common name of an object

are often used together, the common name being in apposition with the proper: thus, in the sentence, "The *steamer Atlantic* has arrived," *steamer* is put in apposition with *Atlantic*.

3. When a noun in the possessive case is in apposition with another, the sign is usually suffixed only to that which immediately precedes the noun limited by the possessive; as, "The poet *Milton's* sonnets."

4. Transitive verbs of *naming, choosing*, etc., are sometimes followed in the active voice by two objectives, the *first* of which is the object of the action expressed by the verb, and the other is put in apposition with it; as, "They elected *him president.*"

5. Words in apposition *must agree* in *case*, but they may or may not agree in *number, person*, and *gender*: thus, in the sentence, "*Thou*, a *man* of wisdom, shouldst know the cause," etc., *thou* is in the *second* person, while *man* is in the *third*.

EXERCISE I.—*Correct* the following sentences:—
MODEL.—"We miss our classmate, he who was so kind."
This sentence is incorrect, because *he*, which is a pronoun in the nominative case, should be in the objective, because it is put in apposition with *classmate*, which is in the objective case. *He* should be *him*, and the sentence should be, "We miss our classmate, him who has been so kind."

1. Respect your teachers, they who do so much for you. 2. His aunt, her who was here, died suddenly. 3. The gardener, him who brought those roses, has a beautiful collection of flowers. 4. Harry, him to whom you spoke, is my friend. 5. I bought Bancroft's, the historian's, last volume. 6. Be kind to your mother, she who loves you so dearly. 7. We should praise God, He who has given us all things. 8. The jeweler, him who repaired my watch, is a good workman.

EXERCISE II.—*Parse* the nouns *in apposition* in the following sentences:—
MODEL 1.—"Franklin, the philosopher, died in 1790."
Philosopher.—*Franklin*, philosopher.—"Philosopher" is a common noun, in the singular number, third person, and of the masculine gender; it is in the nominative case, being put in apposition with *Franklin*, which is in the nominative case, according to Rule V., "A noun, etc."

1. Jefferson, the third President, died July 4, 1826. 2. How he longed for summer, bright and beautiful summer! 3. The steamer Great Eastern

122   RULE VI.—SAME CASE AFTER VERB—NOTES.

arrived at New York. 4. George III., King of England, reigned sixty years. 5. We can not admire some of the poet Byron's writings. 6. His adherents made Cromwell Protector of the Commonwealth. 7. My friend Talbot came to the city with me. 8. He strictly observed his motto, "Prudence." 9. Her youngest brother, Edwin, soon came with his sled, the "Reindeer." 10. We should make our business our pleasure. 11. King Agrippa earnestly listened to Paul the Apostle's preaching.

Her little bird—a poor, slight thing, that the pressure of a finger would have crushed—was stirring nimbly in its cage; and the strong heart of its child-mistress was mute and motionless forever.

RULE VI.—SAME CASE AFTER VERB.

A noun or a pronoun placed after an intransitive verb, or a verb in the passive voice, is in the same case as the noun or the pronoun preceding the verb and meaning the same person or thing.

NOTES.

1. A noun or a pronoun is *after* or *before* a verb or a participle when it *follows* or *precedes* the verb or the participle in the natural order of thought or expression.

Thus, "A *man* he was to all the country dear," in the natural or usual order would be, "*He* was a *man* dear to all the country."

2. The verbs which most frequently separate nouns and pronouns meaning the same person or thing are *be*, *become*, *appear*, *grow*, etc.; and the verbs *call*, *choose*, *consider*, *make*, etc., in the passive voice.

3. If the conjunction *that* is used to connect a finite intransitive verb with a transitive verb preceding, the noun or the pronoun following the intransitive verb is in the nominative case; as, "I think (that) *it* was *he*."

If the intransitive verb is in the infinitive mode and follows a transitive verb which has an object mentioned, the noun or the pronoun following the intransitive verb is in the objective case; as, "I think *it* to be *him*."

EXERCISE I.—*Correct* the following sentences:—

RULE VII.—PERSONAL PRONOUNS—NOTES. 123

MODEL.—"We believed it to be he that spoke to us."

This sentence is incorrect, because *he*, which is a pronoun in the nominative case, should be in the objective, because it means the same person as *it*, which is in the objective case. *He* should be *him*, and the sentence should be, "We believed it to be him that spoke to us."

1. That is him. 2. She does not know that it was them. 3. It is her who is mistaken. 4. Whom do you think it was? 5. It could not have been him who did it. 6. Who do you imagine it to be? 7. I would have done it, if I had been him. 8. "It was me that did it, sir," said the lad. 9. We all thought it to be she.

EXERCISE II.—*Parse* the nouns and the pronouns in *the same case after the verb* in the following sentences:—

MODEL.—"Capt. John Smith became governor of the colony."

Governor.—*Capt. John Smith* became *governor.*—"Governor" is a common noun, in the singular number, third person, and of the masculine gender; it is in the nominative case after the intransitive verb *became*, because it denotes the same person as *Capt. John Smith*, which is in the nom. case, according to Rule VI., "A noun or a pronoun, etc."

1. Thou art the man. 2. He is a hard student. 3. He lived a Christian. 4. I knew it to be my friend. 5. The captives saw that it was a friend approaching. 6. A listening ear, a silent tongue, and a faithful heart are three precious jewels. 7. Truth is a divine attribute. 8. Joseph was made ruler over Egypt. 9. A man he was to all the country dear. 10. His only food was the roots and the berries found in the woods. 11. The falsehood at first appeared to be a truth. 12. "Me" is a pronoun.

Talent is something, tact is every thing. Tact is not a sixth sense, but it is the life of the other five. It is the open eye, the quick ear, the judging taste, the keen smell, and the lively touch; it is the interpreter of all riddles, the surmounter of all difficulties, the remover of all obstacles.

RULE VII.—PERSONAL PRONOUNS.

A personal pronoun agrees with the noun which it represents, in number, person, and gender.

NOTES.

1. A pronoun which represents two or more nouns connected by *and* should be in the plural; as, "Generals *Worth* and *Twiggs* united *their* armies."

RULE VII.—PERSONAL PRONOUNS—NOTES.

Two or more nouns in the singular, connected by *and* and expressing only one person or thing, are represented by a pronoun in the singular; as, "The *traitor* and *renegade* was detested by all that knew *him*."

2. A pronoun which represents two or more nouns in the singular connected by *or* or *nor*, should be in the singular; as, "Neither *James* nor *John* has failed in *his* lesson."

If one of the nouns connected by *or* or *nor* is in the plural, the pronoun representing them should be in the plural; as, "Neither the *father* nor his *children* knew *their* danger."

3. A pronoun in the plural representing two or more nouns or pronouns of different persons connected by *and*, is in the first person if any one of the words which it represents is in the first person; as, "*He* and *I* (*we*) are going to *our* homes."

If none of the nouns is in the first person, the pronoun is in the second person if any one of the nouns which it represents is in the second person; as, "*You* and *he* (*you*) failed in *your* efforts."

4. The pronoun *it* is used to represent a noun or a pronoun in either number, in any person, or of any gender; as, "*It* is *I*."—"*It* was *he*.'—"*It* is *men* that we want, not money."

It is also used indefinitely; that is, without representing the name of any person or thing; as, "*It* snowed all day."—"They roughed *it* in the woods."

EXERCISE I.—*Correct* the following sentences:—

MODEL 1.—"A tree is known by his fruit."

This sentence is incorrect, because *his*, a pronoun in the masculine gender, should be in the neuter, because the noun *tree*, which it represents, is neuter. *His* should be *its*, and the sentence should be, "A tree is known by its fruit."

2.—"Vice and ignorance have cast its blight over thousands."

This sentence is incorrect, because *its*, which is a pronoun in the singular number, should be in the plural, because it represents the two nouns *vice* and *ignorance* taken together and connected by *and*. *Its* should be *their*, and the sentence should be, "Vice and ignorance have cast their blight over thousands."

1. Every body has their faults. 2. If you have committed errors, try

to correct it. 3. He bought some oats and gave it to the horse. 4. If you have a pen or a pencil, lend them to me. 5. He or his brother lost their title. 6. My friend and patron lent me their aid. 7. No one can believe themselves to be free from prejudice. 8. Sugar and rice are brought from warm climates, where it can be raised in great abundance. 9. If a man takes a wrong step, they should not continue in their course.

EXERCISE II.—*Parse* the *personal pronouns* in the following sentences:—

MODEL.—"The songs that my mother sung were the sweetest."

My.—(*Person speaking*) my *mother.*—"My" is a personal pronoun, in the singular number, first person, and of the masculine or the feminine gender, to agree with the noun *the name of the person speaking* which it represents, according to Rule VII., "A pronoun agrees, etc.";—it is in the possessive case, and limits the noun *mother*, according to Rule III., "A noun or a pronoun in the possessive, etc."

1. The farmer cultivates his fields. 2. In a republic the citizens elect their own rulers. 3. O sun, thou who rulest the day, how bright are thy beams! 4. They who suffer most can generally endure the most. 5. I appeal to you, my fellow-citizens, to obey the laws. 6. Through good books good men talk to us. 7. The mountains cast their long evening shadows towards the east. 8. Twilight softens our hearts.

"Alas!" said the sorrowful tree, "my precious robe is gone! It has been torn from me; its faded pieces whirl upon the wind; they rustle beneath the squirrel's foot as he searches for his food. My fair, green vesture is gone. I have lost it, and my glory is vanished."

RULE VIII.—RELATIVE PRONOUNS.

A relative pronoun agrees with its antecedent in number, person, and gender.

NOTES.

1. *Who* is used when reference is made to persons, or to things which are personified; as, "The *judge who* presided, sentenced the criminal."—"Thou *sun, who* rulest the day!"

2. *Which* is used when reference is made to inferior animals, to infants, and to things without life; as, "The *birds which* sing in the groves."—"The *child which* was lost."

Which is also used when the objects composing the unit

denoted by a collective noun are referred to collectively; as, "The *mob which* filled the streets, seemed bent on violence."

3. *That* is sometimes used when reference is made to persons, animals, or things; as, "The same *person that* I knew."—"The first *money that* he received."

That is used instead of *who* or *which* in the following instances:—

I. After an adjective or an adverb in the *superlative degree;* as, "He read the *best* books *that* could be procured."

II. After the adjective *same;* as, "Others share the *same* difficulties in study *that* we encounter."

III. After *who* used interrogatively; as, "*Who, that* indulges in vice, can be happy?"

IV. After the personal pronoun *it* used indefinitely; as, "*It* was he *that* committed the fault."

4. *What* is used when reference is made to things only.

5. *What* is often incorrectly used for the conjunction *that:* thus, "I do not know but *what* it is true," should be, "I do not know but *that* it is true."

6. The rules which determine the number and the gender of the personal pronouns, apply also to the relative pronouns.

EXERCISE I.—*Correct* the following sentences:—

MODEL 1.—" I did not see the man which came."

This sentence is incorrect, because the relative *which* is used to agree with its antecedent *man*, which is the name of a person. *Which* should be *who*, and the sentence should be, "I did not see the man who came."

2.—" Read the best books which can be had."

This sentence is incorrect, because the relative *which* is used after *best*, an adjective in the superlative degree. *Which* should be *that*, and the sentence should be, "Read the best books that can be had."

1. He which was lost, is found. 2. It was he who failed. 3. The cattle who graze upon a thousand hills are mine. 4. It could not have been she who came. 5. Who, who is sinful, can be truly happy? 6. He which pretends to know all things generally knows but little. 7. There is no doubt but what they will succeed. 8. We all admire the habits of the bee, who in summer provides her stores for the winter. 10. See the swallow, who is the harbinger of summer.

Exercise II.—*Parse* the *relative pronouns* in the following sentences:—

Model 1.—"He who is cruel, troubleth his own flesh."

Who.—*He who is.*—"Who" is a relative pronoun, in the singular number, third person, and of the masculine gender, to agree with its antecedent *he*, according to Rule VIII., "A relative pronoun agrees, etc."; it is in the nominative case, being the subject of the finite verb *is*, according to Rule I., "A noun or a pronoun which is the subject, etc."

2.—"I did not hear what he said."

What.—*Did hear* what *said* what.—"What" is a relative pronoun, and in meaning includes both relative and antecedent (*thing which*); it is in the singular number, third person, and of the neuter gender, to agree with its antecedent (*not mentioned*), according to Rule VIII., "A relative pronoun, etc."; it is in the objective case, being the object of the action expressed by the verb *did hear*, according to Rule IV., "A noun or a pronoun which is the object, etc."; it is also the object of the action expressed by the verb *said*, according to Rule IV., "A noun, etc."

1. Avoid those habits which injure the health. 2. Happy is the man whose riches are not of this world. 3. He soon won the prize which was offered. 4. Your esteem is all that I ask. 5. Self-denial is one of the most important lessons that can be learned. 6. The cares, and troubles, and anxieties, which he had suffered, were now past. 7. The bold goddess, whose name is Ambition, and whose dower is Fame, toys with the feeble heart. 8. Avoid what has the least semblance of sin. 9. He is an example of what industry can accomplish. 10. Be firm and honest in every position in which fortune places you.

The selfish boy is one who loves himself only. He does not care whose happiness he destroys, nor whom he deprives of pleasure; all that he desires is to add to his own comfort, and what others suffer from his conduct makes no change in him.

RULE IX.—ARTICLES.

An article relates to the noun which it limits in meaning.

NOTES.

1. *The* can relate to a noun in either the singular or the plural number; as, *The book; the multitudes; the three vessels*

A or *an* can relate to a noun in the singular number only; as, *A book; a* cold *day; an* excited *multitude.*

2. *The* sometimes relates to an adjective used as a noun; as, "*The poor* ye have always with you."

In such constructions the article may also be parsed as relating to some noun understood after the adjective.

3. When several adjectives express different qualities and relate to but one noun, the article is used with the first adjective only.

Thus, "*A* red, white, and blue flag was hoisted;"—this means that *one* flag of *three colors* was hoisted.

The article should be used with each of several adjectives if they relate to the same noun mentioned or understood more than once, and meaning the same person or thing.

Thus, "*A* red, *a* white, and *a* blue flag were raised;"—this means that *three* flags of different colors were raised.

EXERCISE I.—*Correct* the following sentences:—

MODEL 1.—"I would go a great ways to hear him."

This sentence is incorrect, because *a* is used to relate to the noun *ways*, which is in the plural number. *Ways* should be *way*, and the sentence should be, "I would go a great way to hear him."

2.—"He was seated on a black and a white horse."

This sentence is incorrect, because the article *a* is used with each of the adjectives *black* and *white*, both of which express different *colors* or *qualities* of the same thing. *A* should be omitted before *white*, and the sentence should be, "He was seated on a black and white horse."

1. An oats were sown in the field. 2. A bloody pantaloons was found in the woods. 3. A red, a white, and a blue flag is the American emblem. 4. The brown and the gray horse was hurt by the fall. 5. Which is the wider, the Atlantic or Pacific Ocean? 6. The second and third page were lost. 7. John was a good, a respectful, and an obedient pupil. 8. As he walked, he looked neither to the right hand nor left. 9. The good and bad man lived side by side.

EXERCISE II.—*Parse* the *articles* in the following sentences:--

MODEL.—"The poor ye have always with you."

The.—The *poor.*—"The" is the definite article; it relates to the adjective *poor* used as a noun, which it limits in meaning according to Rule IX., "An article relates to, etc."

1. An impatient spirit rendered him unhappy. 2. There the high and the low, the rich and the poor, meet upon the same level. 3. Many a corporal thinks himself a Wellington or a Napoleon. 4. The nominative and the objective case of nouns are alike in form.

There are those who shudder at the approach of autumn, and who feel a light grief stealing over their spirits, like an October haze, as the evening shadows slant sooner and longer over the face of an ending August day.

RULE X.—ADJECTIVES.

An adjective relates to the noun or the pronoun which it describes or limits.

NOTES.

1. Adjectives are sometimes used as nouns, especially when preceded by the definite article; as, "*The rich* are not always *the happiest*."—"None but *the brave* deserve *the fair*."

2. Two signs of the comparative degree or of the superlative should never be used: thus, "The *lesser* evil," should be, "The *less* evil;"—"The *most severest* test," should be, "The *severest* test."

3. An adjective expressing plurality must relate to a noun in the plural: thus, "He was *six foot* high," should be, "He was *six feet* high."—"A chain *ten feet* long."

4. An adjective following a finite verb, and not itself followed by a noun or a pronoun mentioned or understood, relates to the subject of the verb; as, "The *ice* was *smooth*."—"The *snow* lies *deep*."

EXERCISE I.—*Correct* the following sentences:—

MODEL 1.—"The hermit lived in the most strictest seclusion."

This sentence is incorrect, because *most strictest*, which is a double form of the superlative, is used. *Most strictest* should be *strictest*, and the sentence should be, "The hermit lived in the strictest seclusion."

2.—"A pole twenty foot long was used."

This sentence is incorrect, because *twenty*, which is an adjective expressing plurality, is used to relate to the noun *foot*, which is *in* the singular. *Foot* should be *feet*, and the sentence should be, "A pole twenty feet long was used."

1. Iron plates three inch thick were fastened upon the side of the vessel. 2. The court inflicted the most severest punishment. 3. The party traveled but twenty mile a day. 4. The most noblest act of Washington's life was the surrender of his commission. 5. The tree measured eight foot in diameter. 6. The ice on the river was most smoothest. 7. Twenty cord of wood were cut from the hill-side. 8. His position was one of the most pleasantest offered.

EXERCISE II.—*Parse* the *adjectives* in the following sentences:—
MODEL.—"Snow fell to the depth of two feet."

Two.—Two *feet.*—"Two" is a numeral adjective of the cardinal class; it can not be compared; it relates to the noun *feet*, which it limits, according to Rule X., "An adjective relates, etc."

1. The air was soft and mild. 2. The richest rays of the sun rested upon the rough, uneven edges of the clouds. 3. Rome was founded seven hundred and fifty-three years before the Christian era. 4. The wealthy merchant would sometimes leave his palatial residence in the city to visit the little, old, moss-covered cottage in which he had spent his early boyhood days. 5. The well-known snow-bird is a visitant from the frozen regions of the north, coming even from beyond the Arctic circle.

Just then a tall fern, that bowed its graceful head over the brook, seemed to turn into a beautiful, green fairy, and, in sweet tones that sounded like a smaller brook speaking, said: "If, foolish brook, you wish to leave this cool, green shade, the delicate, fragrant flowers that fringe your banks, and your best friends and protectors, these grand old trees; and if your murmuring waves wish to leave these mossy stones and bright, polished pebbles, speak, thoughtless stream, and your wish shall be gratified."

RULE XI.—PRONOMINAL ADJECTIVES.

A pronominal adjective relates to the noun which it limits,—or agrees with the noun which it represents, in number, person, and gender.

NOTES.

1. The distributives all refer to nouns in the singular; as, "*Every day* has its duties."

Either is sometimes improperly used for *each:* thus, "Tall trees lined *either* side of the road," should be, "Tall trees lined *each* side, etc."

2. Of the demonstratives, *this* and *that* refer to nouns in the singular; *these* and *those,* to nouns in the plural; as, This *man,* that *book;* these *men,* those *books.*

Them is often improperly used for *those:* thus, "*Them* acts were unjust," should be, "*Those* acts were unjust."

3. The indefinite *none,* although strictly meaning *no one,* refers to nouns in the singular or in the plural; as, "A book was wanted, but *none* was found."—"Many were examined, but *none* were found qualified."

4. A pronominal is parsed *as an adjective* when the noun which it limits is mentioned; as, "*Each boy* deserved praise."

A pronominal adjective always agrees in number with the noun to which it relates; as, *That* tree; *those* trees; *another* hour; *all* days.

A pronominal may be parsed *as representing a noun,* when it is correctly used without an article, and when the noun to which it refers is not mentioned; as, "*Each* was praised for his conduct."

EXERCISE I.—*Correct* the following sentences:—

MODEL 1.—"Those kind of persons can not be trusted."

This sentence is incorrect, because *these,* which is a demonstrative pronominal in the plural, is used to refer to the noun *kind,* which is in the singular. *These* should be *this,* and the sentence should be, "This kind of persons can not be trusted."

1. Those sort of words provoke harsh feelings. 2. Them keys will unlock either door. 3. These important news has just arrived. 4. He looked up at the beautiful houses on either side of the street. 5. Them are not my sentiments. 6. The messenger who brought them tidings has gone. 7. Those molasses was brought from the West Indies. 8. Throw that ashes into the street. 9. Each stairs lead to the same room.

EXERCISE II.—*Parse* the *pronominal adjectives* in the following sentences:—

MODEL 1.—"That event spread sorrow through the nation."

That. -That *event.*—"That" is a demonstrative pronominal adjective;

I

it can not be compared; it relates to the noun *event*, which it limits, according to Rule XI., "A pronominal adjective, etc."

2.—"The explanation satisfied all."

All.—Satisfied all (*persons*).—"All" is an indefinite pron. adj.; it represents the noun *persons* (understood), with which it agrees, in the plural number, third person, masculine gender, according to Rule XI., "A pron. adjective, etc.;"—in the objective case, being the object of the action expressed by the verb *satisfied*, according to Rule IV., "A noun, etc."

1. Each flower drank in the dew. 2. Enough is as good as a feast. 3. What preparations were made? 4. The vessels were separated by the gale, and several were lost. 5. Much can be done by a careful arrangement of duties. 6. The same feelings of humanity moved the hearts of every one present. 7. Many are called, but few are chosen. 8. This book is all that's left me now. 9. Ah! well do I remember those whose names these records bear. 10. In these times, that which is practical receives the most attention from the public.

Why is it that every one is so much pleased with the common ivy? There is a charm about that plant, which all feel, but none can tell why. Observe it hanging from the arch of some old bridge, and consider how great the interest which it gives to that object; such an interest as but few plants are able to give.

RULE XII.—AGREEMENT OF FINITE VERBS.

A finite verb agrees with its subject in number and person.

NOTES.

1. The pronoun *we* or *you*, even when representing a single individual, requires the plural form of a verb, because the form of the pronoun is plural; as, "John, *you are* in error."

2. A verb in the imperative agrees with the pronoun *thou* or *you* understood; as, "*Go (thou)* to the ant, thou sluggard."

3. A verb, having for its subject a collective noun which suggests the idea of unity, is in the singular number; as, "*Congress holds* its sessions in the national capital."

A collective noun which suggests the idea of plurality requires a verb in the plural; as, "The *clergy were blamed* for the part which *they* took."

4. A verb having two or more subjects connected by *and*,

mentioned or understood, is in the plural number; as, "*Truth, honor,* and *mercy are* noble qualities."

Two or more subjects in the singular connected by *and* and used to denote but one person or thing, require a verb in the singular; as, "That *statesman* and *patriot merits* the gratitude of his countrymen."

When singular subjects connected by *and* are preceded by *each, every, no,* or a similar distributive, they are considered separately, and require a verb in the singular; as, " Every *nerve* and *sinew was strained* to make the effort."

5. A verb, having two or more subjects in the singular connected by *or* or *nor*, is in the singular number; as, " Neither the *time* nor the *cause* of the accident *is known.*"

If one of the subjects connected by *or* or *nor* is plural, the verb should be plural; as, " Neither *he* nor his *friends were* to be blamed."

6. A verb having two or more subjects of different persons connected by *and*, is in the first person if any one of the subjects is in the first person ; as, " *He* and *I (we) are going.*"

If there is no subject in the first person, the verb is in the second person if any one of the subjects is in the second person; as, " *You* and *he (you) are going.*"

7. A verb having two or more subjects of different persons connected by *or* or *nor*, agrees in number and person with the subject nearest to it; as, "Either *he* or *I am going.*"

EXERCISE I.—*Correct* the following sentences:—

MODEL 1.—"Was you there when I called?"

This sentence is incorrect, because the verb *was*, which has the singular form, is used to agree with its subject *you*, which has the plural form. *Was* should be *were*, and the sentence should be, "Were you present when I called?"

2.—"Every nerve and sinew were strained."

This sentence is incorrect, because the verb *were strained*, which is in the plural number, is used to agree with its two subjects *nerve* and *sinew*, which are in the singular connected by *and*, and preceded by *every. Were strained* should be *was strained*, and the sentence should be, "Every nerve and sinew was strained."

3.—"Honor and shame from no condition rises."

This sentence is incorrect, because the verb *rises*, which is in the singular number, is used to agree with its two subjects, the nouns *honor* and *shame*, which are connected by *and*. *Rises* should be *rise*, and the sentence should be, "Honor and shame from no condition rise."

4.—"He or I is to go."

This sentence is incorrect, because the verb *is*, which is in the third person, is used to agree with two subjects of different persons connected by *or*,—*he* in the third, and *I* in the first. *Is* should be *am*, and the sentence should be, "He or I am to go."

1. Was you there when the accident happened? 2. Neither Mary nor her sisters was at the party. 3. "Well," says I, "what does thee think of him now?" 4. The ship, with her crew, were lost at sea. 5. Neither lead nor iron are so valuable as gold, but they is more useful. 6. The news were very discouraging. 7. No whisper, not a sound, were heard. 8. Thou, or he, art to go. 9. Milton's poetry and his prose is vigorous. 10. Such, Mr. President, is my sentiments. 11. Every one have certain peculiar opinions. 12. Cincinnatus is one of the noblest men that is mentioned in Roman history. 13. Six months' service were enough to cure him. 14. Parliament are divided into the House of Lords and the House of Commons. 15. He, and he only, were right. 16. Who does these remarks apply to? 17. Each branch and twig were covered with snow. 18. Has all the boys recited their lessons?

EXERCISE II.—*Parse* the *finite verbs* in the following sentences:—

MODEL 1.—"Henry studies his lesson."

Studies.—Henry studies *lesson.*—"Studies" is a finite transitive verb, regular (pres. *study*, past, *studied*, perf. part. *studied*); it is in the active voice, indicative mode, present tense, and agrees with its subject, the noun *Henry*, in the singular number, third person, according to Rule XII., "A finite verb agrees with its subject in number and person."

2.—"Henry and James study diligently."

Study.—Henry and *James* study.—"Study" is a finite intransitive verb, regular (pres. *study*, past, *studied*, perf. part. *studied*);—in the indicative mode, present tense, and agrees with its two subjects, the nouns *Henry* and *James*, connected by *and*, in the plural number, third person, according to Rule XII., "A finite verb agrees, etc.," and Note under Rule XII., "A verb having two or more subjects connected by *and*, etc."

3.—"If it should rain, I will remain."

Should rain.—(If) *it* should rain.—"Should rain" is a finite intrans. verb, reg. (*rain, rained, rained,*); in the potential mode (used subjunctively), past tense, and agrees with its subject, the pronoun *it*, in the sing. num., third person, according to Rule XII., "A finite verb agrees, etc."

1. Daniel Webster was born in New Hampshire in 1782. 2. Maintain strict temperance in eating and in drinking. 3. The cocoa-tree and the banana bloom in torrid climates. 4. The jury could not agree upon a verdict. 5. Sorrow or joy alone is not our portion. 6. If he conduct himself properly, I know that he will be respected. 7. Never speak for a truth any thing which you know or believe is false. 8. Give me understanding, and I shall keep thy law. 9. He or I am accused of the crime. 10. You or they must go.

As a race, the American Indians have withered from the land. Their arrows are broken, their springs are dried up, their cabins are in the dust. Their council-fire has long since gone out on the shore, and their war-cry is fast dying away to the untrodden West. Slowly and sadly they climb the distant mountains, and read their doom in the setting sun. They shrink before the mighty tide which presses them away; and they must soon hear the roar of the last wave which will settle over them forever.

RULE XIII.—INFINITIVES.

A verb in the infinitive mode depends upon the word which it limits or completes in meaning.

NOTES.

1. A verb in the infinitive mode usually depends upon a finite verb; but it may depend upon another infinitive, upon a participle, or upon any part of speech except the article and the interjection.

2. An infinitive may be used as a noun in the nominative or in the objective case; as, "*To study* seemed his only desire."

3. The auxiliary *to* should not be separated from the remainder of the infinitive by any intervening word: thus, "Be careful *to not disturb* him," should be, "Be careful not *to disturb* him."

4. The auxiliary *to* is usually omitted when the infinitive

follows the active voice of the verbs *bid* (to command) *dare* (to venture), *feel, hear, let, make, need, see,* and a few others; as, "I did not *hear* him (*to*) *speak* on that subject."

To is not omitted after the passive voice of these verbs; as, "The prisoner *was seen to commit* the act."

EXERCISE I.—*Correct* the following sentences:—
MODEL.—" You may bid him to come now."
This sentence is incorrect, because *to*, which is a part of the infinitive, is used after the active voice of the verb *bid. To* should be omitted, and the sentence should be, "You may bid him come now."

1. Let no falsehood to pass your lips. 2. The train was seen slowly start from the depot. 3. Officers were ordered to immediately report to the commander. 4. If a child is bid do a thing, he should be made do it. 5. Although the men suffered much, no one was heard complain. 6. They were heard plan the burglary. 7. Some are able to easily commit to memory long lessons, but they are apt to soon forget them. 8. He durst not to enter without his father's permission. 9. We are bid relieve the wants of the needy.

EXERCISE II.—*Parse* the *infinitives* in the following sentences:—
MODEL 1.—"He hastened to leave the country."

To leave.—Hastened to leave *country.*—"To leave" is a transitive verb, irregular (*leave, left, left*); it is in the active voice, infinitive mode, present tense, and depends upon the verb *hastened,* which it completes in meaning, according to Rule XIII., "A verb in the infinitive mode, etc."

2.—"To live well should be our constant aim."

To live.—To live should be.—"To live" is an intransitive, regular verb, in the infinitive mode; it is used as a noun in the sing. number, third person, and of the neut. gend.; in the nom. case, being the subj. of the finite verb *should be,* according to Rule I., "A noun, etc."

1. The rain began to descend in torrents. 2. Early efforts are known to have been made to find a north-west passage. 3. He learned to read from the signs along the streets. 4. The two friends appeared to be beloved by all that knew them. 5. Washington seems to have taken great pleasure in the chase. 6. Let us never forget how liable we are to err. 7. The children feared that it would begin to rain, and then they would be compelled to remain in the house. 8. He who wishes to be educated, has only to apply his mind properly, and he can not fail to succeed.

You pretend, Mark Anthony, that it is all to protect your person. Is it not far better to die a thousand deaths, than to be unable to live in one's own country without guards of armed men? We must be fenced round by the affections and the good will of our countrymen, not by their arms, if we wish to be secure.

RULE XIV.—PARTICIPLES.

A participle relates to the noun or the pronoun which it describes or limits.

NOTES.

1. A participle may be used as a noun in the nominative or in the objective case; as, "*Reading* good books *promotes* knowledge."—"The morals are corrupted *by reading* bad books."

A participle thus used may be followed by a noun or a pronoun which is the object of the action denoted by the participle; as, "He took pleasure in *doing* his *duty*."

2. A participle preceded by an article or an adjective is a noun simply, and is generally followed by the preposition *of* to govern an objective following; as, "*That* reading *of* the *play* was much admired."

3. The perfect participle, and not the past tense, should be joined with the auxiliaries *have* and *be*; as, "He *has gone* to travel in Europe,"—not, "He *has went*, etc."

4. The perfect participle should never be used instead of the past tense to express simply past time: thus, "James *seen* him do it," should be, "James *saw* him do it."—"He *begun* to read," should be, "He *began* to read."

EXERCISE I.—*Correct* the following sentences:—

MODEL 1.—"By the telling the truth at all times, we may be trusted."

This sentence is incorrect, because the article *the* is used before the participle *telling*, which is used as a noun, and is not followed by *of*. *The* should be omitted, and the sentence should be, "By telling the truth at all times, etc."

2.—"James has saw the whole transaction."

This sentence is incorrect, because the past tense of the verb *to see* is used instead of the perfect part. after the auxiliary *have*. *Saw* should be *seen*, and the sentence should be, "James has seen, etc."

1. He done nothing properly. 2. I have saw him but once this week. 3. The singing the song was postponed. 4. I think that they have all went home. 5. The letter come to the office last week. 6. All her articles of jewelry were stole from the room. 7. Many months were spent in the learning the French language. 8. A very good composition was wrote upon that subject. 9. Vessels run upon the rocky beach, and were wrecked. 10. The ponds and streams were froze during the night. 11. Not many words were spoke upon that subject. 12. Some one has took my cap. 13. Snow has fell to-day for the first time. 14. I did not see the book torn, and I do not know who done it.

EXERCISE II.—*Parse* the *participles*, the *participial nouns*, and the *participial adjectives*, in the following sentences:—

MODEL 1.—"An opportunity neglected never returns."

Neglected.—*Opportunity* neglected.—"Neglected" is the perfect part. of the passive voice of the trans. regular verb *to neglect* (imp. *being neglected*, perf. *neglected*, preperf. *having been neglected*); it relates to the noun *opportunity*, which it describes, according to Rule XIV., "A participle relates to the noun or the pronoun which it describes or limits."

2.—"By observing the faults of others, we may avoid similar ones."

Observing.—*By* observing *faults.*—"Observing" is the imperf. part. of the active voice of the trans. reg. verb *to observe;* it is used as a noun in the singular number, third person, and of the neuter gender; in the objective case, being the object of the relation denoted by the preposition *by*, according to Rule IV., "A noun or a pronoun, etc."

3.—"The earth is clothed in living beauty."

Living.—Living *beauty.*—"Living" is the imperfect participle of the intransitive, regular verb *to live;* it is used as an adjective; it can not be compared; it relates to the noun *beauty*, which it describes, according to Rule X., "An adjective, etc."

1. A few wild flowers, shedding sweetest perfume around, reared their heads in the half-cleared woods. 2. A clambering vine clung to the old oak withered by the lightning's blast. 3. The gray-haired chieftain, having returned from the chase, called a council of his clan. 4. They abandoned the enterprise, having been convinced of its great danger. 5. Let not the evening close upon any day without having added something to your store of knowledge. 6. The hulk, blackened and charred by the

burning oil, floated to the shore, driven by a light breeze blowing from the east.

We were walking in a beautiful grove, from which the wood had been partially cleared; many fine trees were left standing, mingled with the stumps of others long since felled. The mossy roots of those mouldering old stumps are choice places for the early flowers; one often finds the remains of an old oak, or pine, or chestnut, encircled by a beautiful border of this kind, mosses and flowers blended together in a manner which art can never equal.

RULE XV.—ADVERBS.

An adverb relates to the verb, the adjective, or the other adverb, which it qualifies.

NOTES.

1. An adverb should not be used as an adjective, nor should it ever be employed to denote quality: thus, "The *soonest* moment," should be, "The *earliest* moment;" "She looks *sweetly*," should be, "She looks *sweet*."

2. *No* as an adverb can qualify comparatives only; as, "The task *no longer* appeared difficult." Therefore *no* should never be used after *or* to qualify a verb understood: thus, "Will you go, or *no?*" should be, "Will you go, or (will you) *not* (go)?"

3. Two negatives should not be used in the same proposition if a negation is intended; as, "He can *not* do *any* harm," not, "He can *not* do *no* harm."

4. Adverbs should be placed near the words which they qualify. In general, an adverb precedes the adjective or the adverb which it qualifies,—and follows the verb, or is placed between the verb and its auxiliary.

Thus, "He is *truly* happy."—"A *very carefully* written book." —"He fought *nobly*, and he was *nobly* rewarded."

EXERCISE I.—*Correct* the following sentences:—

MODEL 1.—"How pleasantly this breeze feels!"

This sentence is incorrect, because *pleasantly*, which is an adverb, is used as an adjective to describe the noun *breeze*. *Pleasantly* should be *pleasant*, and the sentence should be, "How pleasant this breeze feels!"

2.— "The ship is soon expected to arrive."

This sentence is incorrect, because the adverb *soon* is placed so as to qualify the verb *is expected*, when, properly, it should qualify the infinitive *to arrive*. The sentence should be, "The ship is expected to arrive soon."

1. How beautifully the garden looks! 2. I am glad to see you exceedingly. 3. The oftenest warnings are the most neglected. 4. The penitent lad promised never to commit the offence no more. 5. Velvet feels more smoothly than broadcloth. 6. I am undecided whether to return or no. 7. This peach tastes deliciously. 8. The soldiers appeared finely in their new uniforms. 9. He seemed very badly yesterday. 10. Will you never do nothing to please me? 11. It shall be done at the soonest opportunity. 12. It is like enough that you are wrong. 13. He will never be no wiser.

EXERCISE II.—*Parse* the *adverbs* in the following sentences:—

MODEL 1.—"He answers promptly, for he has been very attentive."

Promptly.—Answers promptly.—"Promptly" is an adverb of manner; it can be compared (pos. *promptly*, comp. *more promptly*, sup. *most promptly*); it is in the positive degree, and relates to the verb *answers*, which it qualifies, according to Rule XV., "An adverb relates, etc."

2.—*Very.—*Very *attentive.—*"Very" is an adverb of degree; it can not be compared; it relates to the adjective *attentive*, which it qualifies, according to Rule XV., "An adverb, etc."

1. The timid rabbit treads softly on the dry leaves. 2. Knowledge can not be stolen from you. 3. He who most blames, is usually most to be blamed. 4. Our duties are not always agreeable. 5. Charles was extremely fond of play, and, though he was rarely punctual at school, he seldom failed to be first upon the ball-ground. 6. Edward could learn easily; if he only read his lesson over once or twice, he could recite it well. 7. He that can not live well to-day, will be less prepared to live well to-morrow. 8. How deliciously cool the air is upon the summit of this breezy hill! 9. I pity the man who has never been wise enough to find out that he has sometimes been mistaken.

That which we foolishly call vastness is, rightly considered, not more wonderful, not more impressive, than that which we insolently call littleness; and the infinity of God is not mysterious, it is only unfathomable; not concealed, but incomprehensible: it is a clear infinity like the darkness of the pure, unsearchable sea.

RULE XVI.—PREPOSITIONS.

A preposition shows the relation between the noun or the pronoun which follows it, and some preceding word.

NOTES.

1. The preposition *to* or *unto* is commonly omitted after the adjectives or adverbs *like*, *near*, and *nigh*; as, "The child is *like* (*to*) his father."—"The Indians came *near* (*to*) the fort."

2. The preposition is often omitted after verbs of *giving*, *procuring*, etc.; and before a term denoting *time*, *place*, or *measure*; as, "He *gave* (*to*) me a book."—"He *procured* (*for*) him a ticket."—"A stream (*by*) *five rods* wide."

3. Care should be taken to use those prepositions which will correctly express the relation intended; as, "I have need *of* your aid," not "— *for* your aid."

In, denoting *situation*, is often improperly used for *into*, denoting *entrance:* thus, "He came *into* the room," not, "He came *in* the room."

Between or *betwixt* refers to two objects or sets of objects only;—*among* or *amongst*, always to more than two; as, "Never hesitate *between virtue* and *vice*."—"*Among* so *many men* it is hard to choose."

EXERCISE I.—*Correct* the following sentences:—

MODEL.—"His opinions are very different to those."

This sentence is incorrect, because the preposition *to* does not express the intended relation between the adjective *different* and the pronominal *those*. *To* should be *from*, and the sentence should be, "His opinions are very different from those."

1. The day being stormy, I staid to home. 2. My brother came in the room. 3. We have much need for your assistance. 4. The dog is very like to the wolf. 5. He was accused with stealing. 6. This pursuit is agreeable with my tastes. 7. The property was divided between the three children. 8. On our trip down the lake we touched in Cleveland and Erie. 9. The city was now in full possession by our troops. 10. I am sorry that you have taken such a dislike for study. 11. Envy is inseparable with greatness.

EXERCISE II.—*Parse* the *prepositions* in the following se: tences:—
MODEL—"The scenes of my boyhood passed before me."

Of.—Scenes of boyhood.—"Of" is a simple preposition; it is used before the noun *boyhood* to show its relation to the noun *scenes*, according to Rule XVI., "A preposition shows the relation, etc."

Before.—Passed before *me.*—"Before" is a compound preposition; it is used before the pronoun *me* to show its relation to the verb *passed*, according to Rule XVI., "A preposition shows, etc."

1. The tops of the hills are white with snow. 2. A good scholar is known by his obedience to the rules of the school. 3. Two young girls were sitting upon the lawn under an elm. 4. We should do every thing for the truth, and nothing against it. 5. Between the eyes and the nose a strange contest arose. 6. A wagon loaded with wheat-sheaves was slowly coming up the lane towards the old red barn. 7. A quick, sharp clang clattered through the heavens, and bellowed loud and long among the hills; presently the storm broke upon us with all its fury.

Generals Worth and Quitman pursued the flying enemy over the causeway, and before night succeeded in gaining possession of the western gates. Santa Anna withdrew his troops in the night, and the next morning the national palace was occupied by the American forces.

RULE XVII.—CONJUNCTIONS.

A conjunction connects the words, the parts of a sentence, or the sentences, between which it is placed.

NOTES.

1. Words connected by conjunctions are of the same class, and are in the same construction; as, "The house is *large* and *handsome.*"—"The city *was attacked* and (*was*) *captured.*"

A noun and a pronoun may be connected; as, "*Mary* and *she* are very studious."

2. A clause containing an adjective or an adverb in the comparative degree, or containing *else, other, otherwise,* or *rather,* should be connected with a clause following by *than;* as, "It is more blessed to give *than* to receive."

3. There is generally an ellipsis in the clause which is connected with a preceding clause by *than* or *as.*

In supplying the ellipsis after *than* or *as,* the second clause should be made to correspond with the first; as, ' He *is* not so far advanced as I (*am advanced*)."—"He is better than James (*is good*)."

4. *As* should not be used for *who, whom,* or *which*, or for *that:* thus, "I saw the man *as* did it," should be, "I saw the man *who* did it."—"He said *as* (*that*) he would go."

EXERCISE I.—*Correct* the following sentences:—

MODEL.—"I could not do otherwise but obey."

This sentence is incorrect, because *but* is improperly used for *than* after a clause containing *otherwise*. *But* should be *than*, and the sentence should be, "I could not do otherwise than obey."

1. Mary had no other excuse but that. 2. The man as came in last was the lecturer. 3. Who else should come but my uncle? 4. The child had no other shawl but the one as she then wore. 5. This conduct is nothing else but folly. 6. The man as robbed the bank was caught by the police. 7. My cousin is not quite so tall as me. 8. I can skate farther and better than him.

EXERCISE II.—*Parse* the *conjunctions* in the following sentences:—

MODEL 1.—"James reads and writes."

And.—Reads and *writes.*—"And" is a conjunction, and connects the two verbs *reads* and *writes*, between which it is placed, according to Rule XVII., "A conjunction connects, etc."

2.—"If it is necessary, I will accompany you."

If.—I will accompany you if it is necessary.—"If" is a conjunction, and connects the two parts of the sentence, *I will accompany you,* and *it is necessary,* between which it is placed, according to Rule XVII.

1. Coal and iron abound in Pennsylvania. 2. The sun shines, and the air is balmy. 3. "You may bend, but you cannot break me," said the reed to the wind. 4. The path of truth is a plain and safe path. 5. If we delay, we will lose precious moments. 6. There is no worse robber than a bad book. 7. I hid myself, because I was afraid. 8. More men drift into error than steer into it. 9. So live that you may not fear to die. 10. Since God has made us to live in society, he designs that we should be helpful to one another.

Good plants and flowers will not be found in a garden unless seed is planted. But weeds will spring up without being planted; and, if they are permitted to grow, they will soon become thicker and stronger than the good plants, and will choke them to death. It is so with the mind:

the soil is good; but angry and wicked thoughts are apt to spring up in it, and, if allowed to remain, they will soon choke the good thoughts, and kill them.

RULE XVIII.—INTERJECTIONS.

An interjection has no grammatical dependence upon any other word.

EXERCISE.—*Parse* the *interjections* in the following sentences:—
MODEL.—"Oh! I am so sorry!"
Oh.—"*Oh*" is an interjection; it has no dependence upon any other word, according to Rule XVIII., "An interjection has, etc."

1. Hurrah! I have a new ball. 2. Bravo! you are a fine fellow. 3. Hist! I hear them coming. 4. Ah! gentlemen, that was a fearful mistake. 5. How soon, alas! he has perished!

GENERAL RULE.

In the expression of thought, those forms and usages of language should be employed which will best express the meaning intended.

NOTES.

1. Every verb should be used with its appropriate form and meaning: thus, "He *set* still," should be, "He *sat* still;"—"The meadows *were overflown*," should be, "The meadows *were overflowed*."

The verbs most frequently misused one for another are *flee*, for *fly*; *lay*, for *lie*; *learn*, for *teach*; *raise*, for *rise*; and *set*, for *sit*.

2. Care should be taken to use that tense which will denote accurately the *relative* time of an action or event: thus, "I *knew* it this long time," should be, "I *have known* it this long time."

3. The indicative present should be used to express what is always true or always false; as, "Galileo proved that the earth *is* round."

4. Such expressions as *had rather, had better, had like, had ought, had as lief,* though in common use, are ungrammatical, and should be avoided.

Thus, "I *had rather* go than not," should be, "I *would rather* go than not."—"I *had like* to have missed the chance," should be, "I *almost* missed the chance."

EXERCISE.—*Correct* the following sentences:—

MODEL 1.—"The men were compelled to fly."

This sentence is incorrect, because the verb *to fly*, meaning *to soar* (as with wings), is used instead of *to flee*, meaning *to hasten* (as from danger). *Fly* should be *flee*, and the sentence should be, "The men were compelled to flee."

2.—"I am twenty-one next June."

This sentence is incorrect, because the verb *am*, which is in the present tense, does not denote accurately the time of the event referred to, which is future. *Am* should be *will be*, and the sentence should be, "I will be twenty-one next June."

1. The dog laid near the door. 2. The child could not set still so long. 3. Winter sat in early. 4. Where have you lain your cap? 5. They had ought to have finished the work much sooner. 6. The wounded deer flew to the lake. 7. I am an invalid these many years. 8. You had better stop if the man tells you. 9. The ancients did not know that the earth was round. 10. I had rather not take it, sir. 11. My mother learned me my alphabet. 12. The tide raises very rapidly in this narrow bay. 13. The teacher said that the sun was the source of light and heat. 14. The steamer was advertised to have sailed yesterday. 15. They would have been very angry if I did not speak pleasantly. 16. I have finished my work two hours ago. 17. It was two years next spring since Mary died. 18. I intended to have gone to-morrow.

GENERAL EXERCISE.

Analyze each sentence, and *parse* each word, in the following extracts:—

THE STREAM OF LIFE.—Life bears us on like the stream of a mighty river. Our boat at first glides down the narrow channel, through the playful murmuring of the little brook and the winding of its grassy border. The trees shed their blossoms over our young heads, and the flowers on the brink seem to offer themselves to our young hands; we are happy in hope, and grasp eagerly at the beauties around us; but the stream hurries on, and our hands are still empty.

Our course in youth and in manhood is along a wider and deeper flood, among objects more striking and magnificent. We are animated by the moving picture of enjoyment and industry passing before us: we are excited by some short-lived disappointment. The stream bears us on, and our joys and our griefs are alike left behind us.

We may be shipwrecked, but we are not delayed: whether rough or smooth, the river hastens towards its home, till the roar of the ocean is in our ears, and the tossing of its waves is beneath our feet, and the land lessens from our view, and the floods are lifted up around us, and we take our leave of earth and its inhabitants, until of our farther voyage there is no witness save the Infinite and Eternal.

 In slumbers of midnight the sailor-boy lay,
  His hammock swung loose at the sport of the wind;
 But, watch-worn and weary, his cares flew away,
  And visions of happiness danced o'er his mind.

 He dream'd of his home, of his dear native bowers,
  And pleasures that waited on life's merry morn,
 While Memory each scene gayly cover'd with flowers,
  And restored every rose, but secreted the thorn.

 Then Fancy her magical pinions spread wide,
  And bade the young dreamer in ecstasy rise;
 Now, far, far behind him the green waters glide,
  And the cot of his forefathers blesses his eyes.

  Toil on! toil on! ye ephemeral train,
  Who build in the tossing and treacherous main:
  Toil on,—for the wisdom of man ye mock,
  With your sand-based structures and domes of rock;
  Your columns the fathomless fountains lave,
  And your arches spring up to the crested wave;
  Ye're a puny race, thus boldly to rear
  A fabric so vast, in a realm so drear.

THE END.

www.ingramcontent.com/pod-product-compliance
Lightning Source LLC
Chambersburg PA
CBHW030359170426
43202CB00010B/1421